NEAL-SCHU

Library Technology Companion

A BASIC GUIDE FOR LIBRARY STAFF

John J. Burke

WITHDRAWN
UTSA LIBRARIES

Neal-Schuman Publishers, Inc.
New York   *London*

In addition to acknowledgments made elsewhere in this book, the author and publisher are grateful to the following sources for permission to reproduce the indicated figures:

Figs. 1–1, 1–2, 1–3 — Photographs courtesy of Christopher Brown-Syed.

Figs. 1–4, 1–5, 4–1, 4–2 — Screen shots courtesy of Innovative Interfaces, Inc. Copyright 2001.

Figs. 3–1, 6–2 — Photograph and screen shot courtesy of Raymond Walters College Library.

Figs. 9–1, 9–2 — Screen shots reprinted with permission of Ai Squared Corporation.

Fig. 9–3 — Screen shot reprinted with permission of R.J. Cooper and Associates.

Published by Neal-Schuman Publishers, Inc.
100 Varick Street
New York, NY 10013

Copyright © 2001 by John Burke

All rights reserved. Reproduction of this book, in whole or in part, without written permission of the publisher, is prohibited.

The paper used in this publication meets the minimum requirements of American National Standard for Information Sciences—Permanence of Paper for Printed Library Materials, ANSI Z39.48-1992.

Printed and bound in the United States of America.

ISBN 1–55570–398–4

Library of Congress Cataloging-in-Publication Data

Burke, John (John J.)
    Neal-Schuman library technology companion : a basic guide for library staff / John J. Burke.
        p.   cm.
    ISBN 1-55570-398-4 (alk. paper)
    1. Libraries—Automation. 2. Library science—Technological innovations. 3. Information technology. I. Title

Z678.9 .B85 2001
025'.00285—dc21   00-062487

Library
University of Texas
at San Antonio

Contents

Contents

Figures

Preface

Welcome to the *Neal-Schuman Library Technology Companion: A Basic Guide for Library Staff.* The world of information technology is an ever-changing one, and this book is intended to help you keep pace. This guide is designed to be an essential resource, whether you are interested in learning the basics about information technology, contemplating adding technology to your library, or need a reference guide to define technology concepts. It covers all of the major types of technologies used in libraries and information centers and addresses issues regarding their adoption and use by libraries: technology plans, security, troubleshooting, buying technology, and more.

I developed the *Neal-Schuman Library Technology Companion* while preparing to teach a course called "Technologies in Libraries." I could not find a single book that covered the broad scope of technologies available to libraries. There were many sources that dealt with library automation, technology planning, or educational technology, but none that tied the three together with guidance on computers, the Internet, and media formats. I was able to find the information I needed for my students, but wanted a single source that could present these concepts as a unit. This is that source.

My goal is that you leave this book with a solid understanding of the basics of information technology and their integration into current library systems. You will understand how to evaluate these technologies and how to assess whether or not to adopt them for your library. You will learn about key technological trends that are influencing the future directions of libraries and information centers. You will learn basic troubleshooting techniques for equipment and software and how to seek more information about this increasingly important skill. I am committed to increasing your level of comfort when speaking about and dealing with the technology you use everyday or will use in the future.

There are sixteen chapters in the *Neal-Schuman Library Technology Companion*. Chapter 1 sets the stage for your consideration of the current state of library technology by examining its history. Chapter 2 discusses sources and strategies for keeping track of technology developments and finding information and advice on existing equipment and applications. The next eight chapters, 3 through 10, give an in-depth look at individual types of technology— from audio technologies to ZIP drives, and from microfilm to the Internet. Finally, the last six chapters, 11 through 16, examine how to plan for, buy, troubleshoot, protect, and design environments for information technology. In addition to serving as a text this book can be used as a ready reference tool whenever you have a specific question on library technology.

Acknowledgments

I would like to thank my wife Lynne and children Madeline and Anna, the students in the Winter 2000 section of "Technologies in Libraries," and my colleagues at the Raymond Walters College Library for their guidance, help, and support in making this book possible. I am grateful to Neal-Schuman Publishers and my editor, Charles Harmon, for their faith in my abilities. Above all, I offer thanks to God for my life and the daily strength He gives me.

Chapter 1

The History of Information Technology in Libraries

The history of libraries is intertwined with the history of information technology. Human societies over thousands of years have produced and relied upon various types of information. Everything from creation stories to herd counts to tax rolls have been recorded, apparently because individuals in these societies saw some purpose in sharing this lore and information with others in the present and in preserving it for future generations. Societies have had to find ways to store and share facts, history, images, data, and fiction as the amount of information continued to increase. Libraries have become a mechanism for accomplishing these purposes and have long played an essential role; were it not for libraries, we would have little or no knowledge of past generations and civilizations.

Handling information requires a diverse collection of practical tools and processes. Today, it is easy to think of information technology as involving only computers or electronic devices. However, we need to remember that the word "technology" includes anything that people create.

Technology, according to the *Oxford English Dictionary*, is a practical or industrial art. (When I hear the phrase industrial art, I always think of high school shop class, in which I (barely) learned the art of shaping wood or metal using specialized tools and following a set pattern.) *Webster*'s definition of technology includes "the application of knowledge for practical ends" and "the terminology of a field." Technology is both processes and products. For the library world, the methods for rebinding books or marking the items in a collection are technologies, just as videocassette recorders or full-text periodical databases are. Information technology as a whole, then, includes any items or methods for containing, transmitting, and storing information.

TRENDS IN LIBRARY TECHNOLOGIES

Two main goals have driven library use of technology: streamlining the workflow of the staff, and better serving the needs of the library's community.

The technologies that have impacted and continue to impact the library world fall into three main groups: (1) those created specifically for libraries and library work, (2) those created within the larger world and then adapted for use in libraries, and (3) those created in the world and brought into libraries without much alteration.

The first group would encompass developments such as Dewey's classification system, the card catalog, and the machine-readable cataloging (MARC) record. The creation of library automation systems and bar-code reading technology, the continuing molding of Internet-based databases to fit library needs, and libraries' own alterations of Website design for internal purposes fit into the second group. We see many examples of the third group in staff use of technology, such as telephones, fax machines, copiers, and many computer applications.

TEN KEY DEVELOPMENTS IN INFORMATION TECHNOLOGY

Many information technologies have been created over the years. The library itself is a technology developed to handle information. Here are ten key developments in information technology that have affected libraries and their work over the centuries, in roughly chronological order. Some of these technologies are still in full use today, whereas others have been replaced. They represent both processes for retaining or organizing information and manufactured tools or other products. All technology is designed to meet a particular need, and while only a few needs ever disappear completely, humanity is always finding new ways to better address long-standing ones. It is important to remember the former roles of these now-obsolete technologies as we look at today's technologies and toward the technologies that may replace them in the future.

Development 1: Writing and Paper

The development of written language and alphabets is the starting place for a discussion of information gathering. Writing's roots can be seen in prehistoric cave paintings— an early pictographic method of communicating information by drawing symbols and pictures to represent words. Pictographs allow individuals to preserve information (at least in the short term) for their own use and also to share it with others. If one writes on something that will last (the next key development in technology for libraries), the information can be passed on beyond the life of an individual and perhaps for many generations.

Compare writing to the other method for passing information along through time: memorization. In many cultures, individuals (called *griots* in West Africa) were able to memorize genealogies, stories, and cultural historic events and recount them as needed. A griot would train someone (usually a child) to memorize the information and thereby would pass it on to succeeding generations. While memorization can be an effective way to contain a set group of information, there are some difficulties with its long-term use.

First, since only one person or a small number of people remember the information, there is the danger of an accident, plague, or untimely death completely wiping out the information. In addition, access to the information is limited, since only that small group can reveal it. Second, since the information is memorized in a distinct pattern, it can be difficult for the griot to recall individual bits of information (the date of a battle or the name of an individual's daughter) without recounting large parts of what they have memorized. Third, despite an exceptional effort, some details are bound to be lost or corrupted through memorization. Even intentional corruption can easily occur, since there is no written record to use for comparison. The safety of, access to, and integrity of the information are major problems that a written record can overcome.

Figure 1–1
Photograph of Papyrus Plants

The physical item that an individual is writing on has a huge impact on how easy it is to pass the information along. There are two key elements of passing information to consider: time and distance. Cave paintings are handy to show to folks who live near you and to share with future generations, but they are awfully difficult to send to a friend in the next valley. The element of transporting information guided the evolution of writing material from cave walls, to stone tablets, to papyrus scrolls (see Figure 1–1 showing papyrus plants), to goat or cow hide (vellum), to linen- and now tree-based paper—a valuable medium, since paper is relatively inexpensive to produce in quantity, is lightweight, and can last for a fairly long period of time.

Development 2: The Printing Press and Books

With a system of writing and a medium to place it on, the communication of ideas could be accomplished relatively easily and cheaply. Paper writings were bound into books (as vellum had been) and passed along. However, the issue of making multiple copies of a work remained a laborious process.

Enter the Gutenberg revolution in the 15th century. The invention of movable type and the printing press (see Figure 1–2) gave people the ability to make their writings available to a larger audience at a much quicker pace. Humanity entered a period in which improvements and innovations changed the publishing process and the audience for books. Printing became faster and faster, paper grew cheaper and cheaper, and literacy increased among the

Figure 1–2
Photograph of Movable Type

populace. These changes set the stage for libraries to develop on a large scale: Many items were being printed, and people wanted to read them. Libraries had existed in earlier civilizations (notably among the Babylonians, Romans, and Greeks) but had only been available to a small elite. Printing allowed information to reach a wider audience and libraries to serve as intermediaries between the growing amounts of literature and a growing literate population.

Development 3: Classification Systems

Libraries have had to deal with ever-increasing amounts of printed materials since the dawn of the printing press. Once the number of books in a library exceeded the librarian's memory, libraries needed a method for locating a specific item or finding materials on a topic. One major breakthrough in organizing and using this information was the development of classification systems.

Unlike today, when libraries tend to choose among two or three "universal" systems, in the past classification schemes were tied to a given library or collection, meeting the local needs of that particular entity. Every library came up with its own way to organize materials by broad categories of knowledge. A tremendous change came about in 1876 with the development of the Dewey Decimal System. Melvil Dewey's subject-oriented system for organizing books caught on and was adopted by a large number of libraries. Today, 95 percent of public and school libraries and 25 percent of academic libraries use the system. The Library of Congress Classification System, developed to organize that library's immense holdings, has been adopted by libraries (primarily academic ones) as an alternative standard. Both systems work on a similar principle: arrangement of the collection by the subject matter of the item.

Classification systems helped libraries tame the growing mass of information. With them, library users could freely browse the collection by topic to find what they needed. The adoption of standardized systems let libraries work together more smoothly and made it easier for patrons to understand how to use multiple libraries. With this innovation in place, libraries could move to make their service more efficient and their users' experiences more fruitful.

Development 4: The Card Catalog

The creation and standardization of a tool to help people locate information in a library was an impressive development in information technology. While libraries had been organized by some sort of classification system for years, the invention of the card catalog in 1791 in France (using the backs of playing cards, which at the time were blank), and the tremendous growth of its use by libraries from the 1850s onward, gave library users an additional tool for finding items beyond browsing the shelves (see Figure 1–3). It enhanced the work of libraries in at least two ways. First, it improved the chances for the library staff to locate materials and therefore to provide service to their patrons. The card catalog allowed the library's collection to be searched from one location without having to browse and scan the shelves. It added convenience as well as the ability to use multiple entry points to access the collection.

Second, the creation of a relatively easy-to-use tool to

Figure 1–3
Photograph of Catalog Card

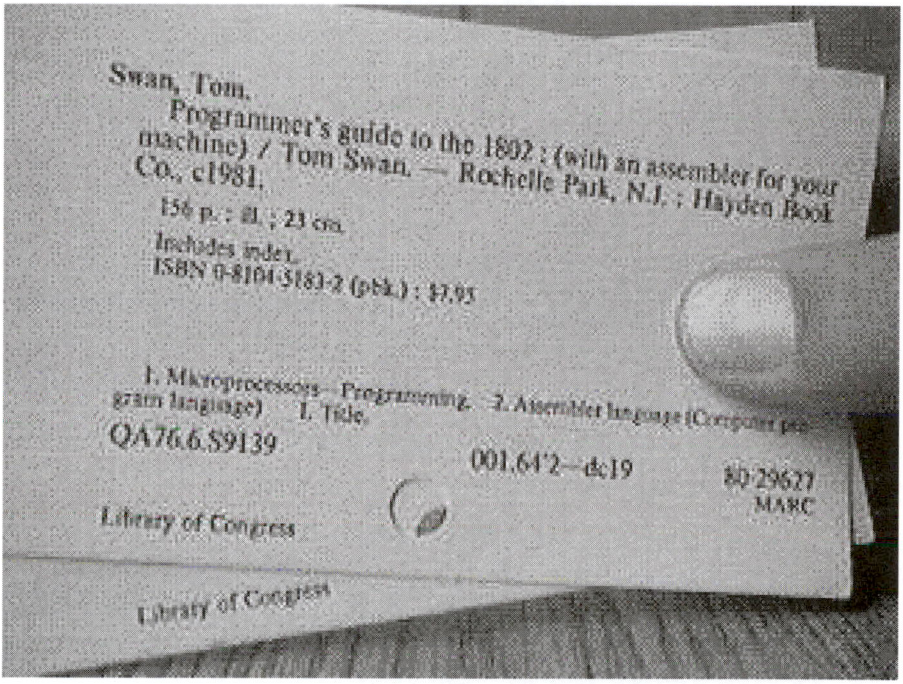

find library information allowed the public to participate directly in the research process. The catalog was relatively simple to use: If you wanted to find books by Louisa May Alcott, you looked in the drawers for the As and then paged through the cards until you found her works. Once catalogs became standardized, it was easy for patrons to walk into any library and see what was available on a subject, or written by an author, or if a given title was held. The card catalog was the first example of an end-user searching tool: The patron gained the freedom to search, and library staff discovered a new instructional endeavor.

Development 5: Library Automation Systems and the MARC Record

With classification systems and card catalogs in operation, libraries were doing a fine job of managing information. There came a point, however, when individuals in the profession saw there could be easier ways to manage large collections of materials and a large number of users. They looked to the power of computers to help make libraries more efficient. Several libraries joined forces with computing professionals in the late 1960s to create the first library automation systems and their descendants, which operated from large mainframe computers and had "dumb" terminals for library staff and users to access the systems. As

Figure 1–4
Screen Shot of Online Catalog Item Record

UCLID   UC's Online Catalog

University of Cincinnati Libraries

| Previous Record | Next Record | Return to Browse | Another Search | Start Over | MARC Display | Export this Record |

Request   OhioLINK Central

You searched: AUTHOR ▾ purcell gary   in View Entire Collection ▾   Search

Record 3 of 3

Author	Purcell, Gary R
Title	**Reference sources in library and information services : a guide to the literature / Gary R. Purcell with Gail Ann Schlachter ; foreword by Charles A. Bunge**
Publish info	Santa Barbara, Calif. : ABC-Clio Information Services, 1984

LOCATION	CALL NO.	STATUS
RWC Reference	Z666 .P96 1984	LIB USE ONLY

Descript'n	xxvi, 359 p. ; 24 cm
Note	Includes indexes
Subject	Reference books -- Library science
	Reference books -- Information science
	Library science -- Bibliography
	Information science -- Bibliography
Alt name	Schlachter, Gail A
OCLC #	10637649
ISBN	0874363551
LCCN	83019700

Figure 1–5
Screen Shot of MARC Record

```
UCLID   UC's Online Catalog

University of Cincinnati Libraries
                    Return to      Another                   Regular
                    Browse          Search      Start Over   Display

001    10637649
005    19850227000000.0
008    840417s1984    cau          00110 eng dnamIa
010    83019700
020    0874363551
040    OKC|cOKC|dORW
100 10 Purcell, Gary R
245 10 Reference sources in library and information services :|ba
       guide to the literature /|cGary R. Purcell with Gail Ann
       Schlachter ; foreword by Charles A. Bunge
260 0  Santa Barbara, Calif. :|bABC-Clio Information Services,
       |c1984
263    8312
300    xxvi, 359 p. ;|c24 cm
500    Includes indexes
650  0 Reference books|xLibrary science
650  0 Reference books|xInformation science
650  0 Library science|xBibliography
650  0 Information science|xBibliography
700 10 Schlachter, Gail A
```

LOCATION	CALL NO.	STATUS
RWC Reference	Z666 .P96 1984	LIB USE ONLY

```
| Welcome | Catalog Menu | Information
```

we will see in chapter 4, these systems allowed libraries to keep track of the items they own and are circulating without a large number of cards and paper (see Figures 1–4 and 1–5). The quest for these systems drove libraries into the computer age, setting the foundation for the world of digital information we see now.

Development 6: Personal Computers

Personal computers (PCs) have made a huge impact on society, including in libraries (see chapter 3). Personal computers increased libraries' computing power and allowed for greater flexibility in choosing the local office and management software than was possible with mainframes. PCs also provided a platform for libraries to experiment with new media types, such as CD-ROMs, and to start accessing remote information services. Today's library would not be possible without the personal computer as a staff workstation and as a method for the public to access library resources.

Development 7: Online Searching

An exciting development of the computer age for libraries was the ability of companies to start computerizing periodical indexes and other resources and then provide them to libraries using a telephone line and a modem. Starting in the 1970s, libraries were able to access resources they could not afford to keep in house and to search these resources much more easily than by paging through their print predecessors. Companies such as Dialog, BRS, and Lexis-Nexis offered libraries access to periodical indexes and full-text newspapers, magazines, journals, and reference sources. Users would choose one or more indexes or periodicals to search and then enter terms to try and find related citations, abstracts, or articles.

The advent of online searching was the first time that libraries had to contend with having resources available that they did not physically own. Connecting to these online services could be expensive (users were charged a set fee per minute), but many libraries were willing to offer this service to their patrons. Early online searching was done by library staff members, partly because the command language for searching was difficult to learn and partly because of the expensive connection fees. Eventually, the methods of searching grew easier (and pricing plans began to change) and library patrons, known as end-users, could more successfully attempt searching on their own. The move toward our current situation of the virtual, online library was underway.

Development 8: Audiovisuals

As with computers, audiovisual items were created within society at large and came to libraries as new packaging for information. Adding new media such as videocassettes and compact discs to the library over the years (see Figure 1–6) changed the complexion of the collection. They also caused challenges for the staff in terms of their shelving, location, and protection. In the past, libraries may have had only the book version of a popular title; today, a library is likely to need to find space for a book, audiocassette, videotape, and perhaps a compact disc version of popular titles. For example, for *Angela's Ashes*, a local li-

Figure 1–6 Timeline of Invention Dates for Audiovisual Items	
Audiovisual Medium	Date Invented
LP records	1948
Audiocassettes	late 1950s
VHS videocassettes	1976
Videodiscs	1978
Compact discs	1982
CD-ROM	1984

The dates are from Walt Crawford, *Current Technologies in the Library: An Informal Overview* (Boston: G. K. Hall, 1988).

brary might have the book, an audiocassette of the book, a compact disc of the book, a videocassette of the movie, a DVD of the movie, and a compact disc of the movie soundtrack. The rich diversity of nonprint formats has allowed libraries to better serve their communities, who expect to have access to a wide variety of media. Their growing inclusion in the collection has caused libraries to rethink their collection development and organization practices and to more readily adopt new media.

Development 9: The Internet

The Internet's impact on libraries is not yet fully realized. Even at this stage, however, it is easy to see that the Internet is causing libraries to rethink how they can deliver services to patrons and how they can supplement and improve upon the information provided online. For example, libraries are answering patrons' reference questions via e-mail in an attempt to assist people no matter the time of day or where they are located. They are working to organize Internet sites and purchase resources to help patrons find what they need. From the early days of library gopher sites and the first Websites to today's online periodical indexes and full-text reference sources, the Internet has become a mainstay of the library world. Libraries can claim many Internet successes yet still face several challenges from this work-in-progress.

Development 10: A Techno-Savvy Populace

Developments in libraries are, and should be, driven in part by the expressed needs and expectations of each library's community, and are major factors impacting technology use in libraries. We have seen in some of the early developments in this list that society often created something new and libraries decided to include it in their collections. This process has been influenced and driven by our patrons requesting items or by people in our communities taking an interest in new media or services before we actually adopt them. Look for the receptiveness of our community to new technology to continue to shape libraries as we confront the issues of e-books and personalized library Websites.

WHAT ARE LIBRARIES USING TODAY?

We find libraries today using a wide variety of technologies. Most have online catalogs and offer public Internet access. Most include a number of different formats for storing information, such as books, periodicals, electronic reference sources, and videocassettes. Libraries as a whole are spending ever more money on electronic resources and the infrastructure needed to support them, often at the expense of traditional, print-based materials. And as libraries invest more in electronic resources, they become less flexible in choosing whether to continue with these expenditures. With this impact in mind, it is crucial for us to understand library technologies in order to help make the right decisions for our library. The rest of this book will look at current library technologies in detail and examine what the future may hold.

SELECTED SOURCES FOR FURTHER INFORMATION

Crawford, Walt. 1988. *Current Technologies in the Library: An Informal Overview*. Boston: G. K. Hall.
Crawford provides an excellent history of the technologies available in 1988, from microfilm to computers.

Musmann, Klaus. 1993. *Technological Innovations in Libraries, 1860–1960: An Anecdotal History*. Westport, Conn.: Greenwood.
An interesting history of library technologies developed, adopted, or adapted during a century of tremendous change for libraries.

Chapter 2

How to Find Information about Library Technologies

Since technology changes at a rapid pace, it is never enough to simply know about and understand the technology owned by a single library. You need to know where you can learn more about technology, whether you are responsible for planning for new technology or are just trying to understand and use what is already in your library. This chapter discusses some places to turn to find answers to technology questions. Knowing where to look for technology facts can be very empowering; it can give you the confidence that you can find an answer. As with reference work, it is more important, and more possible, to know where to look for technology information than to know all the information yourself.

REASONS TO USE TECHNOLOGY INFORMATION SOURCES

There are many reasons in library work to search for information on technologies—both general and library-specific ones. The following are the four most common reasons people who work in libraries search for information on technology:

- *for general awareness*. As noted above, technology is changing rapidly and we need to keep up with current happenings. A library organization can feel overwhelmed by the plethora of new choices on the market and new desires on the part of staff or the community. Library personnel need to have some sense of what is on the cutting edge and how it may apply to libraries. My views on the future of technologies in libraries continue to change based on the information I find and the trends I discover. You may not wish to follow each new development in technology, but you will benefit from using a source of information to keep you abreast of major happenings.

- *to compare products and services*. As libraries try to find technology solutions to fulfill the service needs of their communities, they often need to compare a number of similar products. This occurs when a library is not aware of a product or service to meet its needs, or when a competitive-bidding process is required for purchasing technology. Turning to library colleagues, comparisons in journals, or other sources can be very helpful. Suggestions of specific solutions can then be sought out and evaluated side-by-side to determine the best option.

- *to find a known product or service.* When specific product or service solutions are already identified, a library needs to locate information about them. The information might be descriptions provided by a vendor, critical reviews in formal publications, or the advice and experience of colleagues. Some things that a library may want to find out include: (1) where a product can be purchased, (2) specific pricing information, (3) the success or failure in the use of the item in libraries, and (4) suggestions for alternative products.

- *to configure existing technology.* Once a technology is in place in a library, the questions do not end. Libraries always need more information about installing a product, configuring it to work correctly with other products, and troubleshooting problem situations. There are also times when you want to find out what else you can do with a piece of technology that you bought for a given purpose.

TYPES OF TECHNOLOGY INFORMATION SOURCES

There are many avenues for staying abreast of technological change. The following are the most commonly used methods:

- *periodicals.* A number of periodicals cover information technology that is pertinent to libraries. Since many items of information technology are also used beyond libraries, general-interest technology periodicals can be useful resources, as can general periodical indexes and more specific library indexes (such as Library Literature).

- *Internet sites.* The Internet is a gold mine for technology information. This information may be in the form of vendor Websites, directories of libraries, product reviews, how-to documents, and technology references.

- *online discussions and mailings.* Electronic discussion groups, both particular to libraries and to more general technology issues, can serve as incredible daily update tools as well as forums for specific questions. There are a number of established library groups that are devoted to technology, as well as services that mail out daily tips on software products or Internet search engines that help you refine your abilities. There are also sites that archive earlier discussion groups and Usenet postings and that can be searched for answers to your technology questions.

- *continuing education.* There is no end to what can be learned. While many things can be learned from reading periodicals and searching the Internet, at times a professional development workshop or class can be even better. You can prepare yourself to work with a given technology by participating in a focused continuing education workshop. Other opportunities may give you the chance to get an overview about new developments in technology. There are a large number of workshops and conferences offered every year, and one may well coincide with your current or future needs for technology information.

- *conference exhibits and trade shows.* Gathering technology information would not be complete without visiting the exhibits at a conference or sampling the wares at a trade show. Attending these events are helpful for seeing what new technologies are available and for quickly comparing a number of similar products. There is also the factor of being able to closely examine equipment or software and to ask questions, which is usually not possible over the Internet or by reading a review.

- *visiting libraries.* Finally, visiting a library that has already implemented the technology you are interested in can give you an idea of how the technology will work in your library. Keeping in touch with a network of local colleagues can help you identify libraries to visit. You can contact vendors and ask for a list of local satisfied customers, or pose a question to an electronic discussion group to turn up local or regional libraries that you can visit.

SELECTED SOURCES FOR FURTHER INFORMATION

Periodicals

LIBRARY ORIENTED (TECHNOLOGY FOCUS)

Computers in Libraries. Information Today, Inc. 10 issues per year. $89.95 (U.S.). Website: *www.infotoday.com/cilmag/ciltop.htm* (sample full-text articles are available). Feature articles on applications of computer technologies in libraries and reviews of technology products. Has a very practical focus.

EContent (formerly *Database*). Online Inc. Bimonthly. $55.00 (U.S.) for introductory subscription. Website: *www. ecmag.net/* (sample full-text articles are available). Focused on searching and purchasing electronic library resources and the Internet. Excellent tips and reviews.

Information Technology and Libraries. Library and Information Technology Association. Quarterly. $50.00 (U.S.) (included with LITA membership). Website: *www.lita.org/ital/index.htm* (table of contents and abstracts are available).
Feature articles on applications of information technology in libraries.

Library Hi-Tech. MCB University Press, Ltd. Quarterly. $169.00 (U.S.). Website: *www.mcb.co.uk/lht.htm* (sample full-text articles are available).
Feature articles on emerging technologies in libraries. A bit more research oriented than *Computers in Libraries*.

Library Technology Reports. American Library Association. Bimonthly. $250.00 (U.S.). Website: *www.ala.org/ TechSourceALA/whatisit.html* (summaries of past issues are provided).
Extensive reviews, studies, and testing of various examples of library technology items, from integrated library systems to security products.

Online. Online Inc. Bimonthly. $55.00 (U.S.) for introductory subscription. Website: *www.onlineinc.com/*

onlinemag/index.html (sample full-text articles are available).

Articles, reviews, and product information on databases and other electronic library resources. Also includes coverage of more general library technology issues, such as e-books.

LIBRARY ORIENTED (GENERAL FOCUS)

American Libraries. American Library Association. Monthly (except for combined June–July issue). $60.00 (U.S.) (included with ALA membership). Website: *www.ala.org/alonline/* (full text of news stories and some columns are available).

Magazine for ALA members that includes excellent "Internet Librarian" and "Technically Speaking" columns along with occasional technology-related feature articles.

Information Outlook. Special Libraries Assocation. Monthly. $80.00 (U.S.) (included with SLA membership). Website: *www.sla.org/pubs/serial/io/index.shtml* (table of contents and a free full-text article are available).

Publication for SLA members that includes the technology column "The Cutting Edge" as well as occasional technology-related articles.

Library Journal. Cahner's Business Information. 20 issues annually. $109.00 (U.S.). Website: *www.ljdigital.com/* (full text of news stories and some columns are available).

Articles on various library topics. Noted for its reviews of books, videos, and multimedia products. A number of technology-related columns: "Digital Libraries," "WebWatch," and "Database and Disc Reviews."

School Library Journal. Cahner's Business Information. Monthly. $97.50 (U.S.). Website: *www.slj.com/* (full-text news stories and sample articles are available).
A publication for school librarians that includes regular technology-oriented articles and product reviews.

In addition to the titles mentioned above, the periodical index *Library Literature and Information Science* (H. W. Wilson; more information available at *www.hwwilson .com/NewDDs/wv.htm*) is an excellent resource for finding technology information published in library-related periodicals.

GENERAL TECHNOLOGY

Though far too many to list here, there are a number of good periodicals that may well help with a particular technology information need. They range from computing periodicals such as *Macworld* (*http://macworld.zdnet.com/*) or *PC Magazine* (*www.zdnet.com/zdsubs/pcmag/ shome.html*) to broader technology titles such as *Better Buys for Business* (*www.betterbuys.com*) or *T.H.E. Journal: Technological Horizons in Education* (*www. thejournal.com*). These periodicals and others can be reached using a general periodical index (whatever you have access to) to find product reviews or information on a wide variety of technologies.

Electronic Discussion Groups

Web4Lib (subscription address: LISTSERV@SUNSITE. BERKELEY.EDU; archives: *http://sunsite.berkeley.edu/ Web4Lib/archive.html*)
A very active discussion group that focuses on Web-related technologies but regularly discusses other issues, including public workstation setup and scanning.

SYSLIB-L (subscription address: LISTSERV@LISTSERV. ACSU.BUFFALO.EDU)
A discussion group for librarians involved in systems or electronic resources work. All technology questions are welcome.

LIBSOFT (subscription address: LISTSERV@MAIL. ORST.EDU; Website: *www.orst.edu/groups/libsoft/*)
Discussions of library software issues, from helper applications to integrated library systems.

LM_NET (subscription address: LISTSERV@LISTSERV. SYR.EDU; archives: *http://ericir.syr.edu/lm_net/*)
List focuses on school librarians and school library issues, but many of the discussions have a strong technology focus (particularly electronic resources and educational technology). A highly active group.

There are many other library-related electronic discussion groups, including a large number devoted to specific technologies or products. A good resource for finding others is Library-Oriented Lists and Electronic Serials (*www. wrlc.org/liblists/*). You can also try the more general discussion group search site Liszt (*www.liszt.com*).

Tip and Trend E-mail Newsletters

Current Cites (http://sunsite.berkeley.edu/CurrentCites/)
A free monthly e-mail that contains annotations of information technology articles and other items written by a team of librarians and library staff. An easy way to scan the professional literature for technology-related publications.

Free Pint (www.freepint.co.uk)
A free newsletter that covers electronic business information sources and searching techniques; mailed out every two weeks. While *Free Pint* claims to be devoted to business information, many of the sources are of general interest to those interested in Internet searching. As well, a number of technologies (such as hand-held computers) are discussed that may be of interest to a more general audience.

Edupage (subscription address: LISTSERV@LISTSERV. EDUCAUSE.EDU; archives: *http://listserv.educause.edu/ archives/edupage.html*)
A thrice-weekly, free e-mail that contains summaries of a variety of news stories covering trends and developments in information technology. A nice way to stay in touch with technology happenings beyond the library world.

NewsScan Daily (subscription address: send e-mail to *newsscan@newsscan.com* with "subscribe" in the subject of the message; sample issue available at *www. newsscan.com/*)

A free daily summary of information technology happenings. A well-written source that is similar to Edupage, but offers some interesting historical perspectives on technology and includes some reader commentary in its postings.

Tips from Element K Journals (www.elementk journals.com/zdtips/)
A selection of free, weekly, e-mail tip mailings that you can receive. The mailings are focused on particular software applications (such as PageMaker or Visual Basic) or technology topics (such as Inside the Internet or Weekly Buzz). Each mailing contains a useful tip or selection of news events.

Topica: TipWorld (www.topica.com/tipworld/)
A collection of free e-mail tip mailings that are sent out each business day. The subject matter of the tips range into a variety of areas beyond technology, but there are a number of technology ones available. Very useful tips on everything from viruses to Internet industry happenings.

Dictionaries and Glossaries

Webopedia (http://webopedia.internet.com)
A searchable dictionary of computer and Internet technology terms. A very extensive source that includes a brief definition for each term, along with links to related terms and Websites that offer additional information. A number of entries also include diagrams or images.

CMP's TechWeb TechEncyclopedia (www.techweb.com/ encyclopedia/)
A similar source to the *Webopedia*. Includes lengthy definitions of terms and links to related concepts.

ODLIS: Online Dictionary of Library and Information Science (www.wcsu.edu/library/odlis.html)
An up-to-date dictionary of terms relating to library and information science that includes a number of entries relating to technology. Compiled by Joan M. Reitz of Western Connecticut State University.

Boss, Richard W. 1997. "Glossary." In *The Library Administrator's Automation Handbook*. Medford, N.J.: Information Today.
While a bit dated, this is one of the most extensive glossaries of library and information technology that I have discovered. I would recommend consulting it for clear and concise definitions of common and obscure technology terms.

How-to Documents

ZDNet Help & How-To (www.zdnet.com/zdhelp/)
A collection of guides and documents to help you diagnose computer and technology problems and make choices about hardware, software, and more.

CNET Help.com (http://help.com/)
A collection of guides, documents, and discussions on various information technologies. Offers a variety of methods to find the advice or solutions you need.

Knowledge Hound (www.knowledgehound.com)
   A directory of how-to information sites on a variety of
   subjects. The "Science and Technology" section has a
   number of subtopic areas that list useful guides for computers, the Internet, software, and more.

Dave's Guides (www.css.msu.edu/PC-Guide/)
   A number of helpful guides and documents on buying
   various types of computers and upgrading and troubleshooting them. Put together by the author of the site,
   Dave Krauss of Michigan State University.

Product Reviews and Vendor Information

CNET (www.cnet.com)
   This site includes lots of technology information, product reviews, how-to documents, and advice. A good
   starting place when planning to buy computer and other
   technology items.

IDG.net (www.idg.net/)
   This site has a lot of technology news, but also brings
   together stories on technology developments and information on various types of products. Articles and documents are organized by product or service type.

*Library Automation Resources (www.escape.ca/~automate/
   resource.html)*
   A source list of printed and electronic resources on all
   aspects of library automation. Compiled by Naomi
   Lloyd.

Librarians Online Warehouse (*www.libsonline.com*)
A searchable directory of more than one thousand companies that sell library products. The companies can be browsed by products and services.

Library Automation Vendors (*www.lib.uiowa.edu/cps/automation/vendors.html*)
Links to a variety of lists of library automation companies.

Planning and Building Libraries (*www.slais.ubc.ca/resources/architecture/index.html*)
A collection of links to vendors and projects relating to the construction and equipping of libraries. Compiled by Linda Levar.

You can also find individual vendors through Yahoo! (*www.yahoo.com*) and other search engines.

Continuing Education Opportunities

Librarian's Datebook (*www.hsl.unc.edu/libcal.htm*)
A calendar of upcoming continuing-education events for library staff.

Yahoo! Listing of Library and Information Science Organizations (*http://dir.yahoo.com/Reference/Libraries/Library_and_Information_Science/Organizations/*)
The Yahoo! search directory's listing of various international, national, state, and local library and information science organizations. Handy for finding out about conferences and professional development opportunities.

American Library Association Events (www.ala.org/events/)
   A site listing conferences and meetings sponsored by the
   ALA and its divisions. Also has a "Datebook of Events"
   that lists the future activities of various organizations.

Special Library Association's Strategic Learning and De-
velopment Center (www.sla.org/professional/)
   A calendar and guide to professional-development opportunities offered by SLA.

Chapter 3

Computer Workstations

Computers have become part and parcel of work, education, and entertainment in our society. It should come as no surprise, then, that libraries employ them extensively for public and staff activities. Unfortunately, the inner-workings of this now-common tool are often hard to understand, and many people find computers use to be frustrating. The goal of this chapter is to provide the information essential to helping you understand the basic pieces of a computer and how computers operate. The following chapters on library automation systems (chapter 4), networking and communications technology (chapter 5), the Internet (chapter 6), and electronic library resources (chapter 7) address more specific uses of computers; chapter 12 also discusses securing library workstations for use by the public. This chapter will serve as a guide to the computer itself and its accompanying technology, as well as provide a list of some common library uses for this technology.

COMPUTER ESSENTIALS

Computers are very complex devices that can seem daunting to operate. A few basic points should help you understand computer workstations. Workstations are personal computers, just like ones you may have at home. A workstation consists of a monitor, the central processing unit (CPU, that part of the computer that contains the main components of the system), some input devices such as a

Figure 3–1
Photograph of a Computer Workstation

keyboard and a mouse, and perhaps some peripherals, such as a printer or a scanner (see Figure 3–1).

Every component in a personal computer is plugged into the *motherboard*, a piece of circuitry that serves as the foundation for the workings of the computer. There is a *processor*, which powers the calculations the computer must make to run software and process information. *Random access memory* (RAM) affects the speed and performance of the computer by giving the computer's software "space" to work in while it is running. There are also a variety of *cards* plugged into the motherboard, components that serve specific functions for the computer. These include video cards that allow items to display on the monitor, sound cards that control audio output, and modems that allow the computer to communicate through the telephone network.

Figure 3–2
Table of Computer Storage Media and Their Capacities

Drive Type	Media Type	Media Capacity	Primary Use(s)
Floppy	3.5 in. floppy disc	1.44 MB	Small file storage and backup
CD-ROM	CD-ROM disc	650 MB	Application distribution and use
CD–RW	CD–RW disc	650 MB	ReWritable CD for storage of large files and backups
DVD-ROM	DVD-ROM disc	4.7 GB-17 GB	Application distribution and archival storage
ZIP	ZIP disc	100-250 MB	Removable storage of large files
Tape	Magnetic tape	Up to several GB	Archival storage and backups

Space to store information in workstations comes in two varieties: the RAM is memory space that can temporarily hold the computing processes that software spawns; ROM (read-only memory) contains information that cannot be altered by the user. Storage devices of various kinds are needed for long-term storage and moving software and other files from computer to computer. A *hard drive* typically has the capacity to hold many different software programs and files and serves as an internal storage device. External or removable storage is available in the forms of *floppy drives*, *CD-ROM drives*, *CD–RW drives*, *DVD-ROM drives*, *Zip drives*, and *tape drives* (see Figure 3–2).

Figure 3–3 Computer-related Measurements	
bit:	simplest level of computer information. A bit can have the value of 0 or 1.
byte:	eight bits, which is enough memory to represent a single alphanumeric character.
kilobyte (K):	one thousand bytes; equivalent to a short note on a single sheet of paper.
megabyte (MB):	one million bytes; equivalent to 200-300 pages of text.
gigabyte (GB):	one billion bytes; common measurement of hard drive and storage space.
megahertz (MHz):	common measurement of the internal speed of a computer's processor.
bits per second (bps):	common measurement of data transmision through modems or computer networks.

HOW COMPUTER CAPACITY IS MEASURED

Figure 3–3 contains terms of measurement that are used to express the capacities of computer equipment. Their definitions should help you understand what this equipment can do and how you can compare similar pieces of equipment.

COMPUTER SOFTWARE

The above items are collectively termed computer *hardware*. Hardware includes any physical part of, or addition to, a computer, as well as the complete device itself. Now comes *software*, the programs that make the computer do what we want it to do (and, on occasion, things we were not really planning for it to do). A piece of software is also known as an application or, from older days of computing, a program. There are a variety of types of software available, from games to educational applications to financial management packages. Below are the three most common types found on library computers:

- *management/office products*. Just like any other business enterprise, libraries need to have software to accomplish their work. Word-processing applications (such as Microsoft Word and WordPerfect) can be used for producing handouts, memos, and reports of various kinds. Spreadsheet software (such as Microsoft Excel) is useful for keeping track of budgets and schedules. Database software (for example, Filemaker Pro and Microsoft Access) is handy for maintaining mailing lists and for creating smaller da-

tabases to manage periodicals and other purposes.
- *presentation software*. Libraries that create instructional materials and presentations use presentation software. The software can combine text, still images, clip art, sound, and video to outline and illustrate a lecture that can be projected in a classroom or be used to make brochures or signs. Prominent examples of this software include Harvard Graphics, Microsoft PowerPoint, and Astound.
- *Internet-access software*. Libraries require Internet-access software of various types to make use of the Internet and Internet-based resources, as well as to communicate with others electronically. There are two common types: electronic mail software (such as Eudora Pro and Microsoft Outlook), which automatically connects to the user's e-mail account, and Internet Web-browser software (for example, Internet Explorer, Netscape, and Opera), which connects to a requested site on the Web.
- *CD-ROM software*. CD-ROM stands for compact disc-read only memory. Since so many reference sources have been produced in this format over time, it is common for libraries to have the software to run these sources installed on their workstations. For instance, a library may have *Masterplots* on CD-ROM and keep it on reserve behind the circulation desk for in-house use on a designated workstation. That workstation then has to have a software program installed on its hard drive in order to run and use the CD-ROM. Alternatively, the library could set up the CD-ROM on a network for access by multiple workstations, in which case the software for the CD-ROM

may just need to be installed on the network server (a single workstation).

With the proliferation of books that include CD-ROMs, libraries have a new complication: How will their patrons access these materials? Should libraries load these CD-ROMs (particularly when they are included in reference books) on computers in the library? This can be a difficult process due to the number of sources available. Should they offer to make them available on a case-by-case basis? This requires patron access to an unsecured computer that will allow the installation of CD-ROM software and requires that library staff be trained and comfortable with installing software.

Should patrons only be able to use these products at home on their own computers? Should they be allowed to check out the CD-ROMs at all? While patrons who are truly interested in the source may be able to install the requisite software on their own computer, there are issues to be addressed here. Examples include whether or not our patrons delete that software on their own computers when they return the CD-ROM (in keeping with licensing agreements), and whether we wish to risk damage to the source.

Most CD-ROM use is focused in the public services areas of a library, but remember that staff employ CD-ROM–based resources as well. For instance, the technical manuals for library automation systems may be on CD-ROM and are well-served by being installed on staff workstations. Or there may be staff reference sources that should be accessible within the library (for instance, *Books in Print* on CD-ROM is very helpful in acquisitions and collection-development work). As with sources available from public workstations, these staff CD-ROMs can be set up on a single workstation or networked throughout the library.

OPERATING SYSTEMS

Operating systems provide the environment in which all other software functions in the computer. An operating system (OS) is really just a large piece of software that controls how the computer works, and it has a number of capabilities. It is important to know which operating system you are working with so that you can choose complementary software correctly. In general, an OS is the intermediary between the applications we want to use and the computer's processor, and it makes sure that the processor completes needed operations and that we see the results. An OS allows for *multitasking*, the ability to have more than one application running at the same time and to switch back and forth between them. For instance, you can be connected to the Internet and at the same time be running a word-processing application—and use both applications in turn as needed. An OS also provides the ability to change some characteristics of the *interface* we use to interact with our applications. The interface is what you see on the screen and then manipulate by using the keyboard and mouse (the *desktop* is the interface for Windows, for example).

One of the initial personal computer operating systems was DOS (disc operating system). It still remains with us at the base level of some older personal computers. DOS was primarily a text-based operating system. It was characterized by its command line interface, in which every task you wanted the computer to complete had to be typed out on the screen at the command prompt or included in a program. Graphics could be displayed within programs, but the enduring image of DOS is text on a screen.

A huge innovation in operating systems came with the advent of the Macintosh computer in the early 1980s. Personal computers at the time were called either Apples, after the Apple Corporation that ended up creating the Mac, or IBM-PCs, after the IBM Corporation that produced the first PC (even when other manufacturers produced so-called PC-clones, they were still called IBMs or IBM-compatibles). The Mac stood in stark contrast to the predominant DOS-running IBM PC of the time. The Mac had a *graphical user interface* (GUI) that consisted of a screen with little graphical images (*icons*) that ran programs or opened up additional screens (*folders*) containing additional icons. You clicked on the icons using a device called a *mouse*. The Mac was thought to be more user friendly than the DOS machines and became more and more proficient at displaying and allowing the manipulation of images. This was a revolutionary happening and caused the development of a similar GUI operating system by the Microsoft Corporation called Windows.

The world of operating systems today is still divided between Macs and Windows PCs and their respective operating systems. The Mac is now on the ninth version of its operating system (OS9), while Windows has a variety of versions in use. Windows 98 and 95 are most common, with Windows 2000 and NT found on workstations and servers in heavily networked environments. Windows-based PCs have continued to dominate Macs in sheer numbers (hovering around 80 percent of the market), but Macs still have an edge in graphic design software and image manipulation. We are also seeing the rise of open-source (read "free") operating systems such as Linux as competitors to Windows. It will be interesting to see what developments come next.

THE OPERATION OF COMPUTERS

When you start a computer by pressing its power button and turning it on, it goes through the boot-up process. We might think of this process as an annoying delay before we can actually do something on the computer, but this is when the computer needs to make sure that it has all of its components in order (the RAM, hard drive, and other cards). During boot up, the computer gets the operating system running and brings it to the point where you can select an application. The operating system runs constantly while you are using the computer.

If you wish to turn your computer off, it is important to first follow the correct procedure to shut down your operating system. This allows the operating system to "get its ducks in a row": it can clear out temporary memory space and cleanly shut down parts of its software. Then you can turn off the power. Some individuals will turn off a computer after completing a task with it, while others will leave the computer on forever. The general recommendation that I have for running a computer is to minimize any wasted time that it runs (which somewhat increases your electricity costs) but also to minimize the number of times you turn it on or off (which can wear out the switch on the CPU and stress the operating system). A good rule of thumb is to turn on your computer when you arrive at work and leave it on until you are ready to go home—or until you know that you will not work on it any longer that day.

On occasion a computer may lock up—an application or the entire computer stops working. This can be due to a failure or error in a particular application or within the operating system itself. If you can still use the keyboard to type commands or move the mouse, you may be able to close a malfunctioning application and then reopen it to continue your work. This can happen sometimes if you have multiple applications open (perhaps you are using your word processor and your Internet browser, and the word processor just stops responding to your commands). If the failure is bad enough that using the keyboard or mouse is impossible (that is, nothing happens on the screen when you type or move the mouse), you will have to reboot the computer to straighten out the problem.

COMPUTER PERIPHERALS

The term *peripherals* refers to a variety of computer hardware items that have specific functions. Printers are a very common peripheral in libraries and print everything from budgets to book labels. They come in three main varieties: dot matrix, ink jet, and laser. Laser printers provide the highest quality of printing but are the most expensive. Dot-matrix printers are less expensive and good for printing temporary documents like lists of call numbers and citations or circulation receipts. Ink jets fall somewhere in between the two in terms of cost and quality. Scanners are another peripheral, and have increased in popularity as equipment costs have decreased and interest in digital images has grown. You may also see multimedia add-ons such as speakers and, more rarely, microphones.

MINIMUM STANDARDS FOR NEW COMPUTERS

Minimum requirements for computers, or anything else, are always in the eye of the beholder. What I find acceptable might seem paltry to one person and excessive to another. However, the following criteria may guide you in your computer assessment and purchasing. These aspects of a computer are generally the most important ones to consider at the time of this book's writing (fall 2000):

Processor: PowerPC G4 for Macs; Pentium III for PCs
Clock speed: at least 500MHz
RAM: at least 64MB (128MB would be better if possible)
Hard drive capacity: 10GB or more
Drives: 3.5-inch floppy drive, DVD-ROM drive, and Zip drive or CD–RW drive
Monitor: 17 inch (15 inch will do, but the more screen size the better)
Modem: 56.6Kbps

If your next computer meets these standards, you should be happy with it for about a month or two until the next fast processor or modem or whatever comes out at the same price as you just paid. Realistically, though, since we cannot keep pace with technology, these minimums will keep your computer in good order and able to handle software for a couple of years, which is the minimum many libraries need. Buy the best you can afford at any given moment in time.

SERVERS, MAINFRAMES, AND LAPTOPS

There are many different types of computers out there. This chapter concentrates on workstations because they are found in libraries in the greatest numbers. Computers that host online catalogs or other networked resources are known as *servers* (see chapter 5). In the past, however, before there were true personal computers, large programs or software such as a library automation system required very powerful computers. These computers were often referred to as *mainframes*. They reached out to individual users through *terminals*, devices that consist of a monitor and a keyboard. Let me note here, however, that most libraries have transitioned from using larger computers, such as mainframes, to machines not so unlike an average computer workstation for hosting their catalogs or Websites. We will discuss the nature of servers in chapter 4. *Laptops* are compact versions of workstations that can be easily moved around.

LIBRARY USES FOR COMPUTER WORKSTATIONS

Libraries have found ways to use computers in every facet of their operations. Some uses are primarily available to staff members, while others are used by both staff and the library's public. Even as this book is written, a library somewhere out there is probably adding a new use. At the present time, however, the following are the primary categories of use for computers in libraries.

- *collection control.* Libraries hold the maintenance, organization, and growth of their collections as a major aspect of their missions. As such, the areas of a library organization dedicated to these services have been early adopters of computers. In particular, the cataloging, acquisitions, and circulation operations of libraries have used library automation systems or independent pieces of software to accomplish their tasks. The volume of work in these areas has made them clear targets for automation, as does the fact that they each involve tasks with a fairly repetitive process. Adding records for items to an online catalog, ordering materials from vendors, and tracking circulation and fine information are daily technology tasks for most libraries.

- *interlibrary loan.* The practice of borrowing materials from other libraries and lending owned items existed before the computer age, but computers have made it much easier to locate libraries who own a desired book, video, or periodical article. The management of borrowed and loaned items by computer is also much more convenient than by paper files. While much of the transmission of materials still takes place through the postal service, courier services, or fax, computers have added the ability for periodical articles or book chapters to be transmitted via the Internet.

- *electronic reference resources.* As discussed in chapter 1, the ability to access reference and informational resources remotely strongly impacted libraries over the latter quarter of the twentieth century. Libraries are now providing periodical and reference databases to their communities both from within the library and from individual users' workstations at home or work. The scope and depth of a library's collection can be quickly multiplied by the addition of these resources, provided they are well chosen.

- *Internet access tool.* The Internet has become an important information resource for libraries as well as a medium to connect to electronic resources. It is crucial for libraries to provide Internet access to staff and the public in ways that fit their missions, and for many libraries this means having access to the Internet from a number of public workstations as well as from most or all staff workstations. Having computers available with the requisite peripherals and speed to handle Internet communication is a must.

- *management/office tool.* The computer brings a variety of standard office applications into the library as well. Word processing and spreadsheet software programs are used widely in libraries for creating memos, reports, and budget requests. Libraries have joined the rest of the world in using this software to better track statistics and financial concerns and to prepare print-ready handouts and documents.

SELECTED SOURCES FOR FURTHER INFORMATION

The resources listed at the end of chapter 2 contain more information on the topics covered in this chapter. Product information and further computer concept explanations can be located in the Websites and other resources listed there.

In addition, you can take a look at Dave Anderson's *PC Technology Guide* (*www.pctechguide.com/*) for an introduction and further discussion of PC components and operations. It includes a number of helpful diagrams and easy-to-understand explanations. For those interested in Macintosh information, try *MacDirectory* (*www. macdirectory.com/*). It has links to Mac products and information.

A nice overview of workstation basics and specifications can be found in Michael Kaplan's "Hardware and Network Considerations." (In *Planning and Implementing Technical Services Workstations*, edited by Michael Kaplan. Chicago: American Library Association, 1997, pp. 3–15).

Chapter 4

Library Automation Systems

Library automation systems were devised to computerize a variety of library functions. They are known by a variety of names, including (among others) integrated online library systems (IOLS), online systems, online catalogs, automation, and library systems. Having been the occasion for the first major addition of computers to libraries, these computers are often associated with the terms "automation" or "systems" in libraries, even though these terms really encompass more technologies than just library automation systems. Though not yet found in every library, these systems are continuing to grow in use; there are now thousands of libraries using them throughout the world, and very few libraries should continue to exist without one of some kind (budget permitting).

WHAT IS A DATABASE?

To understand the magic of a library automation system (and many other library resources), it is good to have a sense of what a *database* is. A database consists of a collection of *records*, which are made up of a number of *fields*, each of which contains a piece of information. Databases meet a very serious need: to organize information so that it can be easily searched and retrieved. Computerized databases exist for all sorts of different functions, from managing mailing lists to helping people find full-text periodical articles. I like to think of the card catalog as the perfect model for a database.

If we imagine a card catalog as a database, then each card represents a record. Each card in the catalog contains a standard set of categories of information—author, title, publisher, subject headings, call number, and so on. These categories are analogous to fields, which can contain any information you would like. A database is built on the premise that you can find the individual records that you need for a given purpose, just as a card catalog leads you to individual catalog cards you need to find books or other items in a library. Databases can also be searched by certain fields, much as a catalog can be searched by author, title, and subject. There is one aspect, however, in which an electronic database is much different from a card catalog: there is greater flexibility in choosing among fields to search, and there is usually a keyword option available that can search across multiple fields at once.

A library automation system is the result of converting a card catalog into electronic form. It stands as an individual database, made up of many MARC (machine-readable cataloging) records, each of which contains a number of fields full of information about an item in the catalog. It is searchable by individual fields (author, title, subject, and so forth) and by keyword (which typically allows for a combined search of the author, title, subject, and notes fields of the catalog). Let's now look at some of the different ways a library automation system can be configured.

TOOLS FOR THE TRADE

Library automation systems may be *integrated* or *stand alone*. An example of an integrated system is one that has a module (or software program) to handle an online catalog, and another module to handle circulation, and perhaps a third module for managing acquisitions. All three modules work together and share data between them (for example, the online catalog shows when an item is checked out). This is also called a *multifunction* system. A stand-alone system is one in which there is perhaps just a single module or a combination of nonintegrated modules that do not share data. This situation may be found in smaller libraries that have automated more slowly—adding, say, circulation management first and then deciding to add an online catalog later.

Many stand-alone systems are simply applications that run on a single workstation. Most integrated systems are multiuser systems, which network computers to allow multiple staff members and the public to work simultaneously on and in the system. Library automation systems may be created in house by knowledgeable computer programmers, assembled from a combination of outside vendors' products, or, in the case of most integrated systems, bought as a *turnkey* system from a single vendor. A turnkey is a technology that is set up entirely by the vendor, meaning that you only have to "turn the key" (that is, press the power button) to start it up.

LIBRARY AUTOMATION SYSTEM COMPONENTS

A library automation system contains a number of different modules. Each is designed to handle or provide a different task or service. Not every system will have each of the following modules, but the four discussed below are the most common ones you will find among integrated library systems.

- *Online Public Access Catalog (OPAC).* The OPAC, which allows patrons to search a library's collections, is probably the most well known of the modules,

Figure 4–1
Screen Shot of a Web-based OPAC

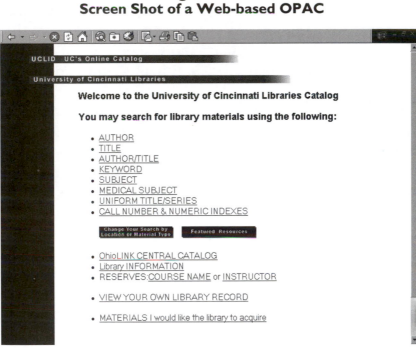

since it is where the public interacts with the library system. For this reason, the design of the OPAC's interface (how one interacts with and navigates the catalog) is crucial. The interface may be a Web or graphical user interface (GUI) (see Figure 4–1), or it may be a text-menu interface. Some libraries have both of these options available, but newer library systems tend to be GUI-only. For many libraries, the OPAC menu also includes links to other kinds of library resources, such as periodical indexes or reference databases.

- *cataloging module.* This module is used to add and modify MARC records in the catalog. Each time a new item is added to the collection, a MARC record for it must be included in the catalog. The records can be created from scratch within the cataloging module, or they can be purchased from a MARC vendor (such as OCLC) and then altered to meet local needs. The first option is known as original cataloging, for which a skilled cataloger examines the item and enters author, title, and publication information into the system and creates meaningful subject headings. The second option is generally known as copy cataloging, and the copied MARC record requires only the addition of a local call number and perhaps other minor modifications.

- *acquisitions/serials modules.* These two modules are actually separate parts of a library automation system, but their functions are rather similar. The acquisitions module is used to order library materials electronically from vendors and then check them into the system as they arrive. The serials module has a check-in function for periodicals that helps the library staff keep track of received and missing issues. The module can also generate claims requests to vendors for these missing issues. Both modules can aid in gathering statistics for the library (the number of items or periodicals available in a given subject area, for example) and financial management (generating up-to-date acquisitions budget figures). These tasks are difficult under a paper-based system.

- *circulation module.* The circulation module handles the many routine operations of the circulation services department (see Figure 4–2). It can be used to check materials in and out and maintain a record of

Figure 4–2
Screen Shot of a Circulation-Module Interface

```
*** INNOPAC -- Copyright 1999, Innovative Interfaces Inc ***
              *** CIRCULATION SUBSYSTEM ***


              O > Check-OUT
              I > Check-IN

              R > RENEW
              H > HOLD an item
              D > DISPLAY the holds on a title

              V > VIEW a patron record
              P > PATRON record maintenance

              A > ADDITIONAL circulation functions
              Q > QUIT

              Choose one (O,I,R,H,D,V,P,A,Q)


              Friday August 11 07:04PM

         1 Sess-1    129.137.142.2              1 18/55
```

when items are due. If a patron wishes to place a hold on an item or have an item recalled, the system can make note of the request and send out recall notices. The module tracks overdue fines and damage charges and can generate bills for patrons. It can also generate overdue notices to mail out to patrons. As with the other modules, the circulation module keeps statistics on the number of items circulated and can keep track of circulation by material type and subject area. Circulation modules allow a library staff to replicate their circulation policies in automated form and have the system automatically set due dates, accept holds, and accomplish other similar tasks.

BENEFITS OF LIBRARY AUTOMATION SYSTEMS

A library automation system provides a number of improvements to library service:

- The system provides users with a wider variety of ways to search for items at the library than does a card catalog. Keyword searching is probably the most obvious addition, but the ability to search by call number or ISBN can also be very handy. The more access points you have to a collection of information, the better your chance of finding what you need.
- An OPAC can motivate patrons to use the library more, or at least attract them to the catalog where they may find a larger number of helpful items.
- An online system can help create a technologically savvy image for the library.

- A library system can allow users to access the catalog remotely rather than just within the library.
- Most systems have the ability to link from the catalog to additional electronic resources (such as periodical indexes). Whether in a text-based or GUI system, this ability allows for the integration of the various electronic resources of the library.
- Once all of the items in the collection have been added to the system, it is much easier to inventory the collection and provide accurate counts of holdings by subject or type of material.
- Many routine tasks are eliminated from staff duties or made easier by the addition of a system. One outcome of this benefit is that books and other materials may well end up on the shelf more quickly.

DISADVANTAGES OF LIBRARY AUTOMATION SYSTEMS

As with anything, there can be drawbacks to a library automation system. Most of the disadvantages revolve around the process of converting from a paper-based system:

- Converting to an online system can be extremely time-consuming and expensive, both in terms of selecting and purchasing a system and in the staff time required to key or copy records.
- The equipment used to operate the catalog is expensive. A card catalog only requires a typewriter and cards, but an automation system necessitates comput-

ers to host the system and for public and staff work-stations.

- The technology can scare some users away if they are not familiar with computers.
- Even though the system eases routine tasks, it ends up creating additional tasks, such as backing up the database and regularly upgrading and testing the automation software.
- The catalog is not always accessible. Whereas a card catalog can only be made inaccessible by closing the library or by fire or other disaster, an online catalog can break down from a variety of causes.
- No matter how easy it is to work with a given system, a deeper knowledge base is required from the library's staff and patrons. Outside technical support is required for the system to keep running.

These issues are all valid ones to consider when making the switch from a card catalog. Once the switch is made, however, the benefits will most likely outweigh any ongoing disadvantages. No library is going to complete the difficult and expensive process to convert to an online system only to find that they do not accrue benefits. There may be some collections out there that can acceptably be left in a card catalog environment, but these are tiny, very specialized ones. What I would hope to see is for smaller libraries to join in cooperative efforts to bring an automated system into a library consortium. This can distribute the disadvantages among the consortium members.

ELEVEN QUESTIONS TO ASK BEFORE PURCHASING A SYSTEM

Life is full of questions, and the process of purchasing a library automation system is no different. The following is a list of issues to consider before you buy.

1. *How big is the collection?* The answer can have a number of effects. First, if your collection is fairly small, you may not really need an automation system to begin with (or a system may be more trouble to set up than it is worth). Second, the size and complexity of a collection can impact the vendor you choose. Some systems can only handle a small threshold of items, whereas others are unlimited in their capacity. You need to take your future growth into consideration here as well.

2. *How many users will there be?* This question will help you decide whether a stand-alone system on a single workstation (with no other OPAC access) will do, or if you must plan for many simultaneous users. You can then decide the type of system and networking set-up you will need, and also how many workstations you should purchase for in-house use. The total size of your library's community should be considered here, rather than just the number you expect will be in the library at any given time. The answer to this question will also impact remote access, as we will see below.

3. *Which modules are needed?* Decide which operations of a library automation system are really needed by

the library. You may decide that cataloging and circulation are essential, but that your existing acquisitions procedures would not transfer well to a particular system's environment. Or, you may decide that a fully integrated system is the only logical choice.

4. *What level and type of remote access is needed?* Aside from your in-house use, will patrons need to access the catalog at other times or from other places? The number of simultaneous users can affect the network configuration you use and the power of your server. Do you expect users will only connect to the catalog via the Internet, or will they also need a straight dial-up connection (these options are discussed in chapter 5)? You need to see what a particular system can support.

5. *What kind of interfaces are needed—GUI, text based, or both?* This is hardly a choice anymore, since most new systems are GUI based. However, if you are expecting to have remote users who are not connecting via the Web or an internal network, you will likely need to have a text interface that they can dial into.

6. *How long will it take to convert the item records for your collection from cards to MARC records?* This is a process known as a *recon*. It involves either manually keying records based on the information on cards, or copying cataloging records from a bibliographic utility (this is something that the library automation vendor can do for you). However you do it, it is bound to be expensive, time consuming, and

possibly quite frustrating. Just keep telling yourself it is absolutely necessary if you would like to have a working system.

7. *Will you weed before converting?* This is a question of process that can have financial implications. You can just convert your entire collection over to the new system and then weed as needed in the future. Some libraries, however, decide that it is worth their while to undertake a major weed in advance of a recon so that they save time in conversion. To weed or not to weed becomes part of the planning process for moving to a new system.

8. *Are you migrating to a new system?* What will it take to do that? In this situation, you already have a working library automation system and are moving to a new vendor's system. Here you need to know how well equipped the vendor is to make this transition for you—for example, have they ever migrated from your existing system to theirs before? The nice part of this situation is that you already have electronic records for the items in your collection. The potential downside is that some records could be lost in the transition.

9. *Can the user interface of the catalog be modified?* How freely can you alter the appearance of your OPAC screens? Can you change help screens to meet local needs? It would be nice if you had full freedom to rearrange screens at will and easily add additional types of searches to meet your needs, but most systems have major limitations in how modifiable they are. The best you can hope for is some ability to ar-

range screen items to your specifications and to adjust the help screens.

10. *Is the staff interface acceptable?* We cannot pay all of our attention to the patron interface without thinking of the view that staff will have of the system on a daily basis. Modification may or may not be possible, so you need to see if the work that staff will use the system for (such as cataloging items, checking out items) can be easily accomplished without extra steps. Then you can compare the process in one system to that in another. Also, is help information easily available? Online help has its ups and downs, but its availability can be more convenient than tracking down the requisite volume of the vendor's automation manual.

11. *Is the system Z39.50 compatible?* Z39.50 is an international standard for electronic information resources that, if implemented, can allow compatible resources to be searched from a single interface. For instance, if you have linked together your OPAC and a periodical index, you can simultaneously search both from a single search blank (say, the keyword search option in your OPAC). This process utilizes a computing process known as *client/server*, in which a piece of software on your computer (the client) can be used to communicate with one or more information databases (the servers) to retrieve information. The clunky part of this is that a specialized piece of client software needs to be available on each workstation you would like to search from (not just a Web browser). Z39.50 can be a useful attribute for your

library automation system if you foresee desiring this kind of searching.

SELECTED SOURCES FOR FURTHER INFORMATION

Breeding, Marshall. 2000. *Library Technology Guides.* Available online at: *http://staffweb.library.vanderbilt. edu/Breeding/ltg.html* [July 14].
A site that includes links to library automation vendors, library OPACs, and lists of articles on library automation trends and topics.

Cohn, John M., Ann L. Kelsey, and Keith Michael Fiels. 1997. *Planning for Automation: A How-to-Do-It Manual for Librarians.* 2d ed. New York: Neal-Schuman.
Outlines the planning process for purchasing library automation systems.

Integrated Library System Reports. 2000. *ILSR Vendors.* Available online at: *www.ilsr.com/vendors/search2.cfm* [July 14].
A site listing links to library automation vendors. Also has a citation listing (with some full-text links) of library automation articles.

Lloyd, Naomi. 2000. *Library Automation Resources.* Available online at: *www.escape.ca/~automate/ resource.html* [July 14].

A source list of printed and electronic resources on all aspects of library automation.

Meghabghab, Dania Bilal. 1997. *Automating Media Centers and Small Libraries: A Microcomputer-Based Approach*. Englewood, Colo.: Libraries Unlimited.
An excellent overview of library automation technologies and the process for automating a library.

Chapter 5

Networking and Communications Technology

Individual workstations have to be able to communicate with other computers in order for library staff and patrons to access electronic resources. Networks, both large and small, are commonly used in libraries to provide access to library automation systems and other shared resources. Modems may be used in libraries to access some remote electronic resources and can be used by patrons to access the library's OPAC and other resources. This chapter explains how networks operate and how computers can communicate using them and devices like modems.

WHAT DO NETWORKS DO?

Networks enable two or more workstations to share resources. In a very simple form, a library might network two workstations to share a printer, making it possible for both workstations to have equal access to one resource, in this case a printer, and avoiding duplication (the need to buy two printers). In a more complex situation, a technical services department might use a network to share several different printers and a number of software applications among all its workstations. A large main library may have three hundred workstations that need to be able to access the same set of applications (such as a word processor, a spreadsheet program, e-mail software). Rather than purchasing and installing the same applications three hundred times each, the staff can network the various applications on one machine (a server, defined below) so that users at all three hundred workstations can get to it. Networks make it very easy to share files, applications, and devices like printers and scanners. They also make it easy to quickly update the software on many machines at once by installing applications on a network server.

NETWORK COMPONENTS

There are a number of items that a network needs in order to operate. In this section, I define and discuss network servers, operating systems and protocols, topologies, and cabling, and explain how all these items come together to form a network.

Network Servers

First of all, there needs to be a *network server* (sometimes called a file server). The server is where the Software or other resources are installed that people wish to access over the network. The server is a computer much like the standard workstation discussed in chapter 3, but a server tends to have more RAM and perhaps a faster processor than an average workstation. The amount of RAM or the speed of the processor depends on what the server is being used for. If a server is used to connect a dozen computers to a printer, it need not have even as much RAM as I suggested for a standard workstation (128MB) and can run even a slower Pentium processor. However, if a server is to be accessed by many individuals out on the Internet and is running very memory-intensive applications (such as sound or video files), it will need a lot of RAM (maybe 512MB) and the fastest processor you can afford.

A library network server might be used for one or more of the following functions:

- to connect to the Internet to be the Web server for the library's Website,
- to be the host computer for the library's automation system
- to be a file server hosting word processing and other office software, along with staff documents and other files
- to be a host computer for CD-ROM or other electronic resources that are networked in house

A library might have several servers in place to accomplish these tasks, or it might not have any servers at all. My own library uses space on our college's server to run our Website and to network applications for word processing and other things. It all depends on the purposes you have in mind for a network.

Network Operating Systems

A network requires a *network operating system* software of some kind. The computer operating systems discussed in chapter 3 all have networking capabilities as part of their makeup. This means that you can run a network from Windows 95 or 98 and MacOS without having to add additional software. There are also specialized network operating systems that are designed to handle networking processes and communications (such as Novell Netware, Windows NT, UNIX, and Linux). Whichever option is used, the purpose of the network operating system is to make sure that everything connected to the network (workstations and printers and whatever else) can communicate and that the use of those connected items can be managed.

One big issue in managing library networks is controlling what individual users can do when they are using the network. There are two main goals: security and flexibility. Security ensures that a particular user can use only the applications or the files they should have access to. Flexibility allows users to sit down at any workstation connected to the network, log into the network server, and access the same resources they would at any other workstation.

The network software allows for each user to log in with a specific username and password. Different profiles can be set up on the network server so that log-in IDs given to staff members access different resources (or give a different type of access to the same resources) from those IDs set up for public workstations. For instance, library staff members will have log-in IDs that let them access the management side (such as circulation, cataloging) of a library automation system from workstations in the staff area, at the circulation desk, and even from public workstations. Public workstations, however, will have default log-in IDs that only let them access the OPAC.

Another facet of network operating systems is that each workstation connected to the network needs to have network operating system software installed. This is relatively straightforward if the network operating system of choice is already the main operating system for the workstation. If not, then an additional software package has to be installed to allow the workstation and server to communicate. In either case, the workstation and its network software need to be configured for this communication to take place. Just to note here, there are methods that let workstations using different network operating systems (or computer operating systems) to communicate, and they involve adding applications on the workstation. Libraries can thus better serve their users by offering MacOS, Windows 98, and UNIX machines the ability to share the same printers, CD-ROMs, and other devices.

Network Topologies

Networks are arranged depending on what topology has been chosen for them. Some common topologies, or architectures, for networks are bus, star, and ring:

- *Bus* consists of a linear arrangement of workstations and devices that connect to a server in a roughly straight line. It requires the least amount of cabling of any of the topologies, because it involves one long strand of cable that workstations and devices are linked into.

- *Star* is configured with the server as a hub at the middle of the network, with workstations and devices radiating from the center in a starlike pattern. All communications must go through the center of the star in order to get from one workstation to another.
- *Ring* links workstations and servers in a large loop. It requires that communications travel around the loop from workstation to server and back again.

The topologies vary in their speed and their cost of cabling. Bus tends to require less cabling and to offer relatively faster connections up and down its central line. The other two require more feet of cabling and can have slower speeds, since communications must always travel through the server (in the star) or follow the loop (in the ring). They may still be good options, however, depending on the purpose of the network. It is also common for these topologies to be combined. For instance, a bus network may link groups of workstations set up in star patterns rather than just single workstations. This can be an effective way to give a group of workstations access to a central printer, for example, and for other groups to have access to their own printer or other devices. Figure 5–1 offers a view of these topologies.

Network Cabling

Finally, but very importantly, the network requires a cabling system so that the workstations and server can be physically linked to communicate with one another. A cable is plugged into the *network interface card* of each workstation on the network. There are a variety of cable

Figure 5–1
Network Topologies

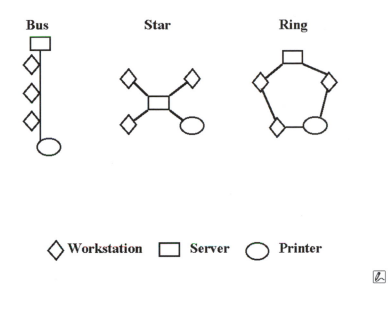

Bus   Star   Ring

◇ Workstation   ☐ Server   ◯ Printer

types and system configurations that a network might use. Some common types of cabling are *unshielded twisted pair* (UTP), *coaxial*, and *fiber optic*.

- UTP is commonly used for networks that exchange data, such as e-mail and CD-ROM resources; category 5 is a popular standard for UTP.
- Coaxial is used mostly for networks that need to transmit big files or video; it is most prominently used for cable television networks.
- Fiber optic is a lightweight, extremely well-transmitting cable that is excellent for data transmission. It tends to be a bit more expensive than UTP, however,

and figures much more prominently in telephone networks than in computer networks.

Putting It All Together

To recap, a library needs seven items for a working network:

1. a network server
2. network operating system software
3. a network topology
4. workstations with network interface cards and network software
5. printers or other devices with network interface cards
6. cabling to tie it all together
7. information resources to share

WHAT'S THE DIFFERENCE BETWEEN A LAN, A WAN, AND A WIRELESS NETWORK?

A LAN (local area network) is essentially what is described above: a server, some workstations, and some cabling. It can involve a dozen workstations or thousands of them. Likewise, there can be a large number of servers involved. Typically, a LAN is a network that is used by a single library or perhaps a single college campus. The requirements of cabling for the LAN make it difficult to extend the network beyond a single organization, because the workstations need to be connected together with the same cable, and it is usually not feasible to bury new cable to connect two workstations that are very far apart.

That is where a WAN (wide area network) comes in. If access to the same resources or applications that are on one LAN must reach people using a different LAN (as in the case of a company with multiple offices), a WAN can be built with devices that allow communication through existing communications networks, such as the telephone network. *Routers* help exchange information between separate LANs, and *gateways* help translate between LANs that use different communication protocols (decided by their choice of network operating system). WANs can then accommodate a larger number of individual users and bring together many more resources for shared use.

Wireless networks use radio signal and infrared transmission technologies to allow computers to communicate with other workstations and network servers without being physically plugged into a cable. Wireless augments cabled networks by giving users freedom of movement and libraries flexibility in arranging stations for networked resources and is a possibility for libraries who find it difficult to rewire the building for a network. A library may use both wireless and cable-networked stations in tandem to give users flexibility. For example, library users can bring in their own laptops or borrow them from the library and use them to type papers or do research from anywhere within the building. It will be interesting to see how creatively libraries and their users make use of this technology.

WHAT'S THE DIFFERENCE BETWEEN AN INTRANET AND THE INTERNET?

An intranet is a single LAN (or a combination of LANs) that is not available to the general public over the network. It is an internal network that is limited to a particular company or organization. It uses Web technology and Internet protocols to give an Internet look and feel to a network. Some larger libraries may have intranets to share staff resources and secure information among library staff.

The Internet is the network to beat all networks. It is the combination of many LANs and WANs spread out worldwide. It uses a special protocol, called Internet protocol, to make it easy for computers using any network operating system to connect to other servers, anywhere. Each server on the Internet has its own *Internet protocol* (IP) number, or address, that allows anyone using the Internet to connect to the server. The Internet also uses a system of *domain names* to give a more memorable look to server addresses (this system allows for names such as *www.yahoo.com* rather than an IP address such as 129.137.146.2).

The Internet is built on very-high-speed phone lines—typically T-3, T-1, and 56Kbps lines—that are dedicated to transferring electronic data. T-3 lines transmit at 43Mbps and form the backbone of the Internet, quickly transmitting e-mail messages, files, and requests to view Web pages from an individual's computer to another computer or server. T-1 lines can transmit at 1.544Mbps and can be leased by organizations (companies, colleges and universities, or individual libraries) who require high-speed connections to the Internet. These organizations can plug a T-1 line into their LAN and afford speedy Internet access to dozens of workstations. Lines at 56Kbps are often leased from telecommunications companies by organizations that wish to provide dedicated high-speed access to the Internet to users (without using modems) through a network.

Most Internet service providers (ISPs) are built on T-1 lines. A user dials into a server at the ISP and accesses the Internet using a portion of that line; the user's access speed is limited by its modem or the connecting device being used. This means that a workstation directly cabled into a LAN that is connected to a T-1 line will be accessing the Internet at speeds up to 1.544Mbps, while a user dialing up from home with a 56Kbps modem will access the Internet at 56Kbps. The ISP is the pathway onto the Internet for the user, but its own connection speed to the Internet is not all passed along to the user. The route an individual or a library takes to access the Internet may look like the diagram in Figure 5–2.

WHAT DO MODEMS, ISDN, AND ADSL CONNECTIONS DO?

Modem technology allows someone with a computer, a modem, and a telephone line to gain access to resources such as the Internet. The modem translates the data the computer is sending into a format, or *protocol*, that can be sent through standard (analog) telephone lines at speeds of up to 56Kbps. Users dial up a modem that is located at a network server, then log in, and then are connected to the server and its resources. Modems can be either inter-

Figure 5–2
Diagram Showing How Individual Computers Connect to the Internet

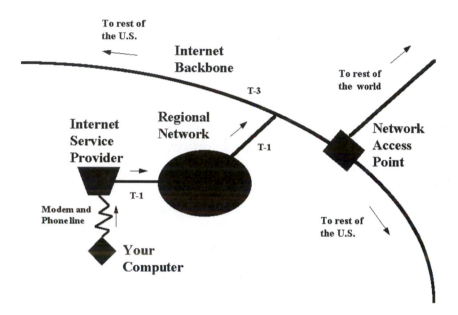

nal or external devices in a user's computer (they plug in as cards). The workstation must have communications software installed to coordinate the translation of requests and information transmitted through the modem.

Users have typically used modems in library contexts to connect to online library catalogs from home or, in libraries in the past, to connect to remote periodical indexes and other resources. Today, most electronic library resources are available only over the Web, not by direct modem connection. That is to say, users dial into an ISP to get to the library's resources, but they cannot dial a phone number at the library to connect to library resources. Many libraries still offer remote access to a text-based version of their catalog via a modem connection. To access Web-based resources, users need to dial into an Internet service provider's server. This requires an Internet service account and thus adds another piece to the remote-access puzzle. Just to note, many libraries still access the Internet themselves by modem rather than by direct connection to high-speed telephone lines.

There are a variety of options for Internet access available beyond using either leased T-1 lines or dialing in with 56Kbps modems. *ISDN* (Integrated Service Digital Network) connections to the Internet use standard telephone lines to provide access speeds of up to 128Kbps. *ADSL* (Asymmetric Digital Subscriber Line) is a very new and very fast method for connecting to the Internet, also using existing telephone lines. It requires a special ADSL modem, which allows a workstation to achieve access speeds of between 1.5 and 9Mbps. *Cable modems* use the coaxial cable laid for cable television to give users access speeds of up to 2Mbps. All of these are somewhat limited for use in that there are only certain areas that have the telephone network or cable infrastructure to support them. Each also requires additional monthly fees to operate them. For those who can get them, they provide fast Internet connections, in some cases equal or superior to a T-1 line.

WHAT DO LICENSING AND PATRON AUTHENTICATION MEAN?

A big issue in all this sharing is making sure that the right resources are shared with the right user (or the right number of simultaneous users). Libraries contract with database providers to let only the patrons of the library use the resources; some licensing agreements limit the number of individuals who can use a database at once. Libraries tend to offer their resources freely to their communities, and this extends to many electronic resources available on their Websites (for example, library catalogs, library collections of Internet sites). When it comes to periodical databases and electronic reference tools, however, libraries need to draw the line at remote access to these services.

There are a variety of ways to conform to licensing agreements and provide *patron authentication*, thereby ensuring that only current patrons of a library are accessing a given resource. One option is to have patrons log in from outside of the library. This gives users the flexibility to connect to the library's Website from any computer. The main downside is that people then have to remember a log-in ID and password, and the library has to make sure to regularly update its lists of valid users with vendors (or in their internal patron systems).

Another method involves providing a database vendor with a range of IP addresses that have been assigned to workstations in a library or an educational institution. Anyone who tries to access the database from a workstation with the correct IP addresses gets in; all other users are kept out. This is easier for users in that they do not need to remember log-in information to get in, and it works well for libraries with many different in-house workstations. The trouble comes with providing remote access to users at home, who need to somehow have their IP address conform to the accepted list of IPs. Universities and other organizations get around this situation by giving users accounts that, when a user dials into them from home, make the user's workstation appear to have an acceptable

IP. Public libraries are not usually able to offer such accounts to their broader clientele.

WHY DO WE HAVE COMMUNICATIONS TECHNOLOGIES IN LIBRARIES?

Networks, modems, and the Internet give libraries the ability to provide a number of services. Library LANs give staff access to local office applications and the Internet and give patrons in-house access to CD-ROMs and other networked resources such as printers, which may also use networked charging systems to assess printing fees to patrons. Modems allow users to dial into library catalogs and to access their ISPs so that they can reach library resources from home. Libraries may also use modems for their own Internet access—or dedicated high-speed telephone lines or other methods. Once on the Internet, libraries can share their resources on the Web and provide access to vendors' Web-based resources.

SELECTED SOURCES FOR FURTHER INFORMATION

Bielefield, Arlene, and Lawrence Cheeseman. 1999. *Interpreting and Negotiating Licensing Agreements: A Guidebook for the Library, Research, and Teaching Professions*. New York: Neal-Schuman.
Guidance on understanding and negotiating licensing agreements for software and electronic resources. A crucial issue for networked resources of all kinds.

DeCandido, GraceAnne A. 2000. "PLA Tech Note: Wireless Networks." *Public Library Association*. Available online at: *www.pla.org/technotes/wireless.html* [April 28].
This is an overall explanation of wireless networking. The site also provides links to vendors, case studies, and other related resources.

Howden, Norman. 1997. *Local Area Networking for the Small Library: A How-to-Do-It Manual*. 2d ed. New York: Neal-Schuman.
Howden gives a detailed introduction to setting up a LAN and understanding networking concepts.

Meghabghab, Dania Bilal. 1997. *Automating Media Centers and Small Libraries: A Microcomputer-Based Approach*. Englewood, Colo.: Libraries Unlimited.
Chapter 7 of Meghabghab's work provides some helpful additional details for the topics covered in this chapter.

The CDROMLAN electronic discussion group is an excellent resource for questions about library networking issues, particularly those that involve sharing CD-ROMs. You can search the group's archives (and find subscription information) at *http://listserv.boisestate.edu/archives/cdromlan.html*.

Chapter 6

The Internet

The Internet is a global computer network that has revolutionized communications and information exchange. Originally developed for military research use in 1969, the "Net" has grown into an entity used by hobbyists, educational institutions, businesses, and just about anybody. As the Internet has grown in commercial and social applications, it has become more important for libraries to provide access to it and to use it themselves for information gathering and provision. This chapter includes basic facts on this worldwide network, and information on how libraries are using it.

A SNAPSHOT OF THE INTERNET

The Internet started as a secure conduit through which researchers working on military research projects could share information over long distances. The U.S. military also wanted the network to function even if some of the connected computers were, say, destroyed in a nuclear attack.

The result was a worldwide collection of host computers using high-speed telephone lines to share information. The military research focus gradually gave way to more general use by academic researchers; as the number of educational and then business users grew, the Internet took off as virtually a public utility in the early 1990s. Individuals with no ties to education, business, or the military were able to get online and tremendously increased the number of Internet users. The U.S. government turned over its operation of the host computers that routed Internet communications—the Internet "backbone"—to private telecommunications companies. The Net continued to grow.

The Internet is now a huge collection of computers and information that is tapped into daily by millions of people. It is a mixture of services and information that is available to a growing percentage of the population, yet inaccessible to society's poorest members except through public institutions like libraries. There is serious money at work in the Internet, as the stock market rise of dot-com companies and the search for e-commerce opportunities intensifies for all businesses. It is also a haven for less financially rewarding, but no less valuable, activities such as recreational chatting, support groups for those in crisis, and exchanging professional advice. There is a freedom to the Internet: the freedom to communicate, to search out information, and to share things. As one might expect, there are sometimes conflicts when this sharing happens, as when recording companies and musicians sue those individuals who place audio files of songs online without paying royalty fees.

So what is the Internet? It is in many ways a reflection

of the rest of the world, and as such is valuable to libraries and individuals seeking information about that world.

WHAT CAN YOU DO ON THE NET?

The answer to this question grows longer each year as new
software and services become available. There are, however, three main things we can do on the Internet: communicate, locate information, and share files.

- *communicate.* It is an exciting prospect: the ability
  to exchange thoughts, requests, and answers with

Figure 6–1
Screen Shot of an E-mail Message

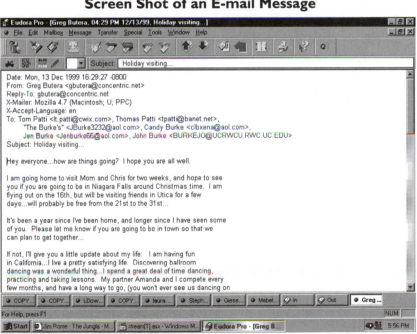

people located all over the planet. Electronic mail is the most common method of online communication, and the one with roots back to the Internet's beginning. It allows users to type and send messages back and forth between individuals or among a group of Internet users via an electronic discussion group (see Figure 6–1). Chat is a more interactive means of communication where users type brief messages to one another in real time, in which users gather electronically at a set location and communicate on a given topic or whatever is on their minds. Other modes of communication on the Internet resemble e-mail, but they are more public. Usenet newsgroups and Web bulletin boards allow interested parties to exchange static messages in a public forum. Like chat, these forums are organized by topic.

- *browse for information.* Active information sharing is accomplished through the communication methods mentioned above. Passive sharing of information online is primarily through the World Wide Web. With browser software, Internet users can "visit" the millions of documents available on Websites. Each site has an URL (or uniform resource locator; for example, *www.neal-schuman.com*) that a user can enter into the browser to connect to the site. The sites are created using hypertext markup language (HTML), a versatile and relatively easy tool that helps create useful pages on the Web. Anyone can place information on the Web, and there is a great mixture of organizational and personal information available. Though the Web can be characterized as passive, its graphical images of all kinds, sound and video clips, and more make it much more than just a presentation of staid, text documents.

- *share files.* While e-mail and the Web get the most attention from Internet users, the ability to share files is a crucial aspect of the Internet. Individuals can send word processing documents or graphics files back and forth for collaborative or informational purposes. Software companies can place demo versions of their products on a Website and allow people to download them to their computers to try them out. While a lot of information on the Internet is available in online discussions or on Web pages, it is easy to overlook the mountains of facts contained in files of various formats.

WHY DO LIBRARIES USE THE INTERNET?

Libraries have come to rely on the Internet just as other kinds of institutions and organizations have. Despite some apprehension on the part of librarians who were not comfortable with computer technology or who wondered if the Internet would replace libraries, libraries have found the Internet to be well-suited to aid and reinforce many of their activities and services. There are five basic ways that libraries use the Internet:

1. *to market themselves and to provide services.* The primary way that libraries do this is through a library Website (see Figure 6–2). Libraries place information about their services, contact information, and organized lists of resource links on their sites. Since the

Figure 6–2
Screen Shot of Library Website

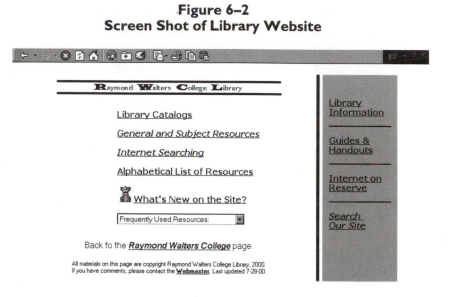

Web is used so heavily as a marketing tool by the rest of the world, it is sensible for libraries to also do so. In addition, libraries are providing actual services over the Internet: Reference service is offered to patrons using e-mail and Web-based forms, and materials requests can be received the same way, as can requests for instruction sessions.

2. *to communicate with each other, with colleagues, and with patrons.* Staff can consult with colleagues in other libraries about equipment needs, service policies, and reference strategies, among other things. E-mail gives staff another way to make contact and pass information along to fellow staff members. It is quick and easy enough that it may well encourage staff to send a message about a new reference tool or a catalog upgrade that would otherwise not have been sent. Since e-mail can easily be sent to a large

group of people, it's also easy to get the word out to everyone. Staff will also receive more e-mails from members of their communities as patrons use e-mail more and libraries continue to market themselves on the Web.

3. *to search for information.* Libraries need to help guide users to the best information sources for their need, and the Internet should be seen as a supplement to the other electronic library resources we provide for our staff and patron use; it can serve as a first, last, or middle source in search strategies for reference questions. Library users are already using the Internet as a source for locating information, sometimes in preference to libraries. We need to accept that sometimes the Internet is the best source and make sure that we can guide people in its use.

4. *as a platform for providing access to resources.* A Website is the most logical way for libraries to offer access to their resources, since a growing number of subscription and free resources are accessible on the Web. In fact, many resources that may have been available in other formats (print or CD-ROM) may now only be available on the Web. Libraries have adopted Websites as the method for giving patrons what libraries hope is a useful organized listing of electronic resources. Some libraries incorporate print resources (and their call numbers) along with the electronic sources to further integrate their reference collections.

5. *to research service methods and product information.* There are a lot of resources on the Internet for finding information in these areas: As mentioned above,

libraries can turn to colleagues for advice on methods and practices; there are discussion groups for every type of library and specialty within libraries; there are sources (see chapter 2) for product information. In addition, most library vendors have Websites to use for surveying their products and contacting them.

INTERNET ISSUES FACING LIBRARIES

Nothing in this world is without its problems. The Internet had brought a lot of good into the world of libraries and our patrons, but there are some issues that we cannot overlook. The first issue is one alluded to above: Some of our patrons are dependent on the Internet for information, often to the point of ignoring libraries. This problem has two aspects: First, our patrons (especially those who already ignore the library) need to be educated on the merits of particular library resources for meeting their needs; second, we as library staff cannot fall into the trap of beating down the Internet in order to raise ourselves up. The Internet needs to be treated by everyone as just another information resource, better at some research needs but worse at others.

An interesting part of this issue are the sites and services on the Internet that offer to answer people's informational questions. Some of these are free sites that link users to experts in various fields who will answer questions related to their expertise. Others charge a fee or let information providers bid on answering questions. It will be interesting to see how profitable these services become, and even over a year. The CD-ROMs could be placed on stand-alone workstations or be networked for multiple stations or even multiple libraries.

Networking a CD-ROM brought in its own expenses, however, as libraries had to pay extra fees to give multiple users access to the resource. Libraries could make a CD-ROM available to a set group of workstations (perhaps six networked computers within the library) or to a certain number of concurrent users across a larger network (as in the workstations of an entire college campus). CD-ROM resources are still around and are utilized most often for reference sources. With the availability of the internet as an access mechanism, though, pay-by-the-minute fees have evolved into subscription costs based on er headcounts. Libraries now pay to connect an entire rary and its workstations, or to handle a certain number of simultaneous users in the library's community who nect via the Web. Users no longer need to be on a lo- etwork to gain access to the resource; as long as they ffiliated with the library or its parent organization, an access the huge network of the Internet. The s in communications technology have made using sources much more flexible for staff and patrons

RAPHIC UTILITIES

, we discussed the efficiency created by the use tomation systems and the dependence of these IARC records. These records are not all cre- dual libraries as they need them. Rather, they

more interesting to see if they provide a valuable service to those who use them.

The next issue involves patrons viewing certain materials within the library (particularly sexually explicit sites). Some might add to this behavior the tendency of patrons to use public access workstations to chat and transmit personal e-mail. Both activities can be offensive to some staff and patrons: the first activity to those staff and patrons who do not wish to view the objectionable material; the second (which is frustrating for staff) to patrons who have to wait to use a workstation. Technological solutions for both cases have involved software that attempts to eliminate access to potentially offensive Web sites and/or programs that block access to some protocols like chat or e-mail.

Some libraries have chosen—and others have resisted—installing filtering software (programs that attempt to restrict access to offensive sites). The software does not necessarily work as it should, however, and can block sites without any offensive content. However, without some steps taken (ranging from user education to filtering), children and others in libraries are able to find or are forced to see images they would rather avoid. The American Library Association opposes mandatory filtering (see *www.ala.org/alaorg/oif/filtersandfiltering.html*) on First Amendment grounds. Many librarians support the use of filters, however. There is no easy answer to this situation, and neither unadulterated access nor filtering is without its casualties. It is an issue that libraries will continue to face for some time.

SELECTED SOURCES FOR FURTHER INFORMATION

If you are interested in seeing some examples of what libraries are doing on the Internet, take a look at the following Websites:

Dowling, Thomas. 2000. *LIBWEB: Library Servers via WWW.* Available online at: *http://sunsite.berkeley.edu/Libweb/* [July 14].

Leeds, Kathy. 2000. *Innovative Internet Applications in Libraries.* Available online at: *www.wiltonlibrary.org/innovate.html* [July 14].

For a list of companies providing reference services online, see:

Sloan, Bernie. (2000, April 5). *WEB4LIB* "Electronic reference and the 'competition.'" Available online at: *http://sunsite.berkely.edu/Web4Lib/archive/0004/0072.html* [2000, October 20]

Chapter 7

Electronic Library Resourc

For our purposes, electronic library resources
range of information sources used by librar
trons. They are the end (the Internet) access
(networks and modems). These services
major reason libraries own computer w
are the foundation for today's electro
brary. This chapter describes the ty
sources used by libraries and the in

The resources listed below may
variety of means, although the
access today is via the Web.
sources were available only th
A library would use a works
nect to a database or an
eral different databases (
versions of the database
which helped libraries
(an annual fee plus a
CD-ROM users we
could cost less tha

are largely available from bibliographic utilities—companies that maintain large databases of MARC records and make them available to subscribing libraries. One example of a bibliographic utility is the Online Computer Library Center (OCLC), which provides a variety of services to libraries. Its central purpose, however, is to maintain a huge computer database of MARC records for published, recorded, and electronic items. These records are created when items are purchased and cataloged by the Library of Congress and the other member libraries of OCLC. Libraries contribute their records to the database and then are able to copy them into their online catalogs. It is a tremendous example of how sharing the effort of keeping track of millions of published items helps ease workloads and also makes it possible for the public to find out where to locate a given item.

PERIODICAL REFERENCE TOOLS

Periodical indexes like the *Reader's Guide to Periodical Literature* were among the first electronic reference sources. It is quick and easy to search for article citations in a database by specific fields or by keywords. Add in abstracts and links to full-text articles and these sources become even more convenient for and valuable to library users. Such "one-stop shopping" for articles is possible from a workstation in the library or at home. Some excellent examples of general and subject-specific periodical databases are those provided by the ProQuest, Infotrac, and EBSCO services.

The current situation represents a drastic change from

the periodical research process of ten or fifteen years ago. Then, it was a time-consuming process that involves flipping through annual volume after annual volume. When I was in college, I would thumb through printed indexes such as *Reader's Guide* or *Social Sciences Index* to find articles that would work for my topic. Those indexes were arranged in alphabetical order by subject heading, and there were times when it was hard to choose the right heading. Once I found citations for articles, I had to determine whether my library owned the periodicals they appeared in by consulting a printed volume that alphabetically listed all of the periodicals and gave their locations in the library. Then I would head to the periodicals area of the collection or up into the stacks (depending on which periodical I was after) to track down the correct issue. In some libraries you had to fill out a request slip for each periodical so that the staff could bring the issue to you (patrons were not allowed to browse the issues by themselves). Then I would head over to the photocopying area and start the slow process of copying each article. The situation today is Nirvana by comparison.

FULL-TEXT REFERENCE RESOURCES

Just as the availability of full-text articles makes research easier, online access to reference sources is a boon to a library's community. Once again, improved searching is an advantage, as is regularly updated material. Sources—which most often are standard references—range from almanacs and directories to encyclopedias and literary criticism collections. Indeed, some libraries switch over to an electronic version rather than buying a new edition of a print source, though others maintain both print and electronic copies of a source.

Full-text electronic reference sources are exciting for their multimedia aspects, such as their ability to bring in sound (listen to Nelson Mandela speaking rather than read his words) and video (watch the human immune system attack a virus in a computer model) to help users appreciate and understand the material. An added appeal is their wide availability, bringing the full-text, image-bearing source to workstations throughout a library and perhaps into the user's home.

ACQUISITIONS TOOLS

Libraries have turned to electronic means to select and purchase items. The process of ordering books and other materials from vendors has automated over time along with other library services, and vendors today are providing sophisticated, Web-based systems for browsing through their catalogs, setting up collection-development profiles, and placing orders. These systems can be used by single or multiple users at an institution; faculty members at colleges and universities can even have access to the systems to make suggestions for purchases. Some examples of these systems are the GOBI (Global Online Bibliographic Information) system of the Yankee Book Peddler company (*www.ybp.com/gobi.htm*), Blackwell's Collection Manager (*www.blackwell.com/services/cm/CM.html*), and Academic Book Center's Book Bag (*www.acbc.com/bkbag/bkmain1.htm*). These systems join long-standing (and now electronic) sources such as *Books in Print* (*www. booksinprint.com/bip/*) and newcomers to the online book information and ordering business such as Amazon.com (*www.amazon.com*).

AUTOMATED- AND META-SEARCH SOFTWARE

This category of electronic library resource is highly attuned to the capabilities of the Internet and the growing networking of information resources. There is software available that can be configured to search a variety of databases all at once. For instance, you could have an option available on your Website for users to simultaneously search your OPAC, a number of periodical databases, a locally held collection of electronic documents, and the Internet at large. While there are certainly situations where such a meta-search (that is, searching a large number of sources all at once) could prove confusing to users because of the large number of results it could produce, there are research needs for which a one-stop search option would save the time of the user. Tying together intranet-, Internet-, and vendor-based resources gives libraries a way to integrate their resources so that users have a fuller picture of what a library has available. To get a sense of what this sort of tool can do for a library, take a look at Intelliseek's Bullseye product (*www.intelliseek.com*), a similar piece of software called Copernic (*www.copernic.com*), or Infotrac's Total Access (*www.galegroup.com/pdf/facts/ita.pdf*).

ADVANTAGES AND DISADVANTAGES OF ELECTRONIC LIBRARY RESOURCES

We have already looked in this chapter at some positive reasons for utilizing electronic information sources. Below are advantages and disadvantages to these resources and their use, not all of which apply to each category of resource. These lists provide the reader with background information that will help in the next section's discussion of some overall issues raised by these resources.

Advantages

- Electronic resources can be easier to search than print because they offer more varied search options. They are also more efficient to use because no paperwork is involved.
- Electronic resources provide services that are not duplicated in other formats (such as the searchable MARC databases of bibliographic utilities or the integration of full-text articles within periodical indexes).
- Electronic resources are more accessible than print; for example, they can be used by multiple users at the same time and can be made available remotely to the library's community.
- Using electronic resources can save space in libraries (using full-text online periodicals rather than microfilm or bound periodicals or electronic reference sources in place of reference books).
- These resources are less costly to access in the long run and are easier to update.

Disadvantages

- Electronic resources can be prohibitively expensive for some libraries (they certainly require libraries to carefully examine what they are getting before they subscribe).
- The resources can stop working at inopportune times.
- They can be difficult to browse through (keyword searching brings up only exactly matching items, as opposed to flipping through a periodical index or reference book).
- Electronic resources may not be exact replicas of existing print versions or may lose information sources over time (especially in the case of full-text periodical resources, which may lose the rights to provide certain periodicals).

ADDITIONAL ISSUES

The pluses and minuses above may help you choose between print and electronic sources. In some situations, though, you may not have a choice: There are no print-based MARC vendors. Still, even when you really do not have a choice, there are still some issues that these resources raise that must be taken into account.

Canceling Print Sources

When we have, either by design or accident, replaced some of our print sources with electronic ones (reference books or periodicals), it will probably occur to someone to cancel the print version. This happens quite frequently with periodical databases or with source aggregators like Lexis-Nexis, which includes a variety of full-text periodicals and reference sources in its databases. This can certainly save money, but if the source is ever removed from the electronic resource, we may end up with a gap in our collection. In libraries where the current version of a source is used to the exclusion of any earlier ones, the impact of this loss may be small. However, in other situations, missing a year (or two) of a heavily utilized periodical title can be disastrous and confusing to patrons ("Why don't you have 1999?"). Remember that your subscription to an electronic resource does not guarantee that it will remain the same over the course of the subscription (to be fair, many resources improve their electronic versions over time).

Access and Licensing

There are a variety of issues to concern ourselves with when we consider the access we wish our community to have to a resource. Multiple-user access tends to be the norm for most resources, but you need to consider where to provide access from (just the library? classroom use? home use?), who to provide access to (everybody? faculty only? library card holders?), and how to make sure that only designated patrons can get into the resource (known as authentication). Authentication is crucial for remote access, because the licensing agreements you sign when subscribing specify your responsibility for ensuring that only authenticated users are using the resource. It can be accomplished by having users log into the resource (providing a user number—library card number, student number, or the like—and a PIN number) or by identifying users by the IP address of their computer.

Another access issue beyond meeting licensing requirements is a technological one: What components does a library or individual need to access the resource? This can include the speed of an Internet connection, the minimum characteristics for a computer workstation, the version numbers of the Internet browser software, and the speed of a workstation's CD-ROM drive. You need to be aware of the minimum requirements for a resource both for equipping in-house workstations and for deciding whether enough of your patron base can use the resource remotely. A library also needs to make enough workstations available to accommodate users. For staff-oriented resources, remember to budget to upgrade staff workstations.

Cost

Cost can be a potential minus of electronic resources. In some cases, electronic resources can be bargains for a library when compared to purchasing the print resource or resources an electronic source includes. This can stand out in the case of full-text periodical resources, where you might cancel a print subscription as well as the microfilm for a title, realizing substantial savings. There are, however, some electronic resources that will require that you maintain your print subscription to the same source for a certain amount of time, thus forcing you to pay twice for the same item, so consider carefully whether an electronic resource will be a feasible expense. Beyond the subscription cost, you also have to take into account the staff time involved in updating software or loading updates to the database itself. In the case of databases that are maintained on a library's own server, the time can differ from resource to resource.

Organizing and Integrating

Libraries have long focused on bringing disparate resources together and organizing them so that they can be found and used. The question libraries now face is: How can we put electronic and print sources together so that they can be used effectively without one type or another getting lost? On the staff side, libraries need to arrange electronic resources on the staff desktop so that they are easy to find. Staff must also understand where and when to use print resources and where and when to use electronic ones, as well as how to lead patrons to the best source, not just the easiest one to find on the shelf or the Website. The issues on the public side of electronic resources are much the same. When we arrange electronic resources on our library Websites, how can we be sure to lead our patrons to print sources when they are the best ones to use? Online pathfinders for a given topic that list electronic and print sources side-by-side can help (for example, the Ohio State University Libraries' Gateway to Information— *www.lib.ohio-state.edu/gateway/*).

Training and Education

Training is crucial to the successful use of electronic resources in a library. If patrons do not understand how (or when) to use the resources, and if staff join them in this ignorance, the library will have wasted a lot of money and not have served its patrons. Any implementation of electronic information sources needs to be accompanied by intensive staff training, part of which should teach staff members how to educate patrons who have questions about the new resources or are encountering them for the first time. This should be done in addition to any formal public instruction program the library may have. Remember that resources can only be used effectively and live up to their potential if those who use them know what they are doing.

In general, electronic library resources force a library to ask some hard questions about its provision of services. When we move from print to online, we need to know what we will do when the resource is not available (what is our backup plan?). We need to consider how providing full-text resources will change what is printed in the library and how many reams of paper we will start using in a month (or a day). The good thing is that electronic library resources can expand the choices our patrons have. The difficult element is that as we add these resources, we grow more and more dependent on resources we have little control over and barely any ownership of. This is the present and future of libraries.

SELECTED SOURCES FOR FURTHER INFORMATION

Cassell, Kay Ann. 1999. *Developing Reference Collections and Services in an Electronic Age: A How-to-Do-It Manual for Librarians*. New York: Neal-Schuman.
An excellent source that outlines the electronic resources available for reference use in libraries and describes the issues these sources raise for reference methodology and staff and patron training.

Kuntz, Jerry. 2000. *LibraryLand: Reference: Commercial Database Vendors*. Available online at: *www.*

librarylandindex.org/ref/data.htm [July 14].
A list of vendors of electronic library resources.

Ohio State University Libraries. 2000. *Gateway to Information.* Available online at: www.lib.ohio-state.edu/gateway [July 11].
An example of the integration of electronic and print electronic reference sources. Worth looking at to get an idea of what sources are available online.

Online Computer Library Center, Inc. (OCLC). 2000. Available online at: *www.oclc.org* [July 14].
OCLC's Website, which can give you a fuller background and description of their services.

Technical Services Unlimited. 2000. *Publishers, Vendors.* Available online at: *http://tpot.ucsd.edu/TSU/publishers.html* [July 14].
A long list of publishers, database vendors, and materials distributors.

Chapter 8

Methods for Storing Information

As noted in chapter 1, there came a point in history when people needed to find a way to share and safeguard information. The quest began with oral history and memorization and evolved through ever-new ways to record information. As this chapter will illustrate, people are still finding new ways to contain information and pass it along, creating new types of media. We need to understand and be able to use these different media because libraries, as repositories of information, are bound to see a wide variety of formats. Aside from accessing them and making them available to our patrons, we need to be able to preserve them (or the information in them) for the future.

PAPER

Despite the long list of formats that follow, paper is still the predominant means for sharing written information and still images. Libraries are still buying, shelving, and circulating the thousands of books and ever-growing number of periodicals published each year. Unlike many of the media that follow, the technology of printing on paper has not changed drastically over the last century. The materials for printing have grown cheaper, which has had some bad effects on preservation, but nothing incredibly innovative has happened when we compare this format to the others. Paper is currently a constant for libraries, and it is too early to suggest that its demise is near.

MICROFORMATS

Microformats are fairly traditional formats for libraries, having existed in some form since the turn of the twentieth century. They consist of rolls or single sheets of photographic film with miniaturized images of pages of text or graphics. The rolls are known as microfilm and the sheets are microfiche. Microfilm can accommodate between 1,000 and 1,500 pages per 100 foot roll of 32mm film (the standard size used in libraries); microfiche can hold between sixty and ninety-eight pages per sheet in its standard format (there are versions called ultrafiche that can hold larger numbers of pages). Libraries use them primarily for routine storage of periodicals and special collections of documents (government documents have often been distributed on microfiche in the past). Both types of microformats require special reading equipment to view them. There are separate readers available for each format, but many microfilm reader/printer units can also be used to view and print microfiche.

COMPACT DISC TECHNOLOGY

Compact disc (CD) technology, invented in the early 1980s, has been used for two purposes: recording high-quality sound (compact discs) and providing a stable source for recording data (compact disc–read-only memory, or CD-ROMs). Both types are widely available, and each one has overtaken an existing media format: compact discs have killed off records and dominate audiocassettes for recorded music, and CD-ROMs have largely replaced floppy discs for distributing software. Libraries include both types in their collections. CDs are borrowed by music lovers and CD-ROMs may be available with children's software and various other applications. CD-ROMs, the primary format for the "multimedia" craze of the early 1990s, are often available in libraries as reference source containers (encyclopedias and other tools). They are also included with books to hold supplemental material.

The technology consists of round, 5.25-inch discs that are pitted by lasers to retain data. CDs can hold a maximum of seventy-four minutes of recorded sound, and CD-ROMs can contain up to 600MB of computer data—unfortunately, CD-ROMs are not very good carriers for video because they cannot play it back quickly enough. CD players and CD-ROM drives are quite common in society and are also found in libraries (most computers come with a standard CD-ROM drive). There are now CD-RW (ReWritable) drives and blank discs on the market on which computer users can record their own music or data in the CD format.

DVD TECHNOLOGY

DVD (which actually stands for nothing, but you will hear digital versatile disc or digital video disc) technology is relatively new on the scene, dating from the late 1990s. It is very similar to CD technology in that it is the same size as a CD, uses a laser-pitting process to place information on the discs, and comes in multiple formats. When we look at those formats, though, we can see the differences between DVDs and CDs. Audio DVDs can hold 50 hours of sound, DVD-ROMs can hold between 4.7 and 17 GB of data, and DVD-video can hold between 2 and 8 hours of high quality audio and video. DVDs can be single or double sided. DVD is a tremendous improvement over CD technology in terms of quantities of data, sound, and video, but it is also a revolution in terms of the speed at which the discs can be played—up to nine times the speed of CDs. The speed issue is what allows DVD to exist as a video-storage format and a potential challenger to videocassettes.

DVDs require a separate drive or player. DVD players can be hooked up to televisions or stereo systems (or a combination) to play the audio and video formats, and DVD-ROM drives to computers, with a nice feature: they also play CD-ROMs. DVD provides a tremendous new media format that has great potential in many areas. Libraries currently need to be ready for DVDs in at least two formats: DVD-video, already growing in popularity, should be added to video collections, which means that libraries that provide viewing stations will need to add DVD players to their arsenals; and, libraries purchasing new workstations should consider including DVD-ROM drives, looking ahead to greater use of this format for software distribution, multimedia application use, and archival storage.

DATA STORAGE OPTIONS FOR WORKSTATIONS

So many of the methods for storing information covered in this chapter are formats that we find on the library shelves (such as books, videocassettes, and CDs). But where do all of the files that make up a full-text periodical index physically sit? Generally, they are placed on server hard drives. This is true for almost every document on the

Figure 8–1
Photograph of Various Types of Storage Media

Internet: files are sitting on hard drives and are backed up to other forms of *magnetic media*. With so many electronic library resources today existing on library servers, vendor's Websites, or elsewhere on the Internet, we need to discuss magnetic media as a storage method.

Magnetic media storage devices use electrical impulses to inscribe information in a certain pattern on magnetic material. The material is encased in a container of some kind that can then be accessed by the same device to retrieve the information. Hard drives, floppy discs, Zip discs (and other kinds of removable storage), and magnetic tape—all magnetic media—are storage devices that suit particular purposes. A variety of storage media are assembled in Figure 8–1.

Hard drives most often store operating systems, installed software applications, and working or archived files that will be used on a given workstation. Current hard drives can contain several gigabytes of data. They can crash or lose files, but tend to be pretty safe for data because they stay in one place and are not removed or touched in any way. They are also very convenient to use—it is quick and easy to save and retrieve files on them.

Floppy discs are good for moving smaller files around, for running small back ups, and for distributing smaller software applications. The once standard 5.25-inch floppy (which was relatively flexible hence the name "floppy") has been replaced by a 3.5-inch model that is hard plastic. Though there is not much room on a current floppy (only 1.44MB) when you compare it to other media formats, this is still enough to store word processing documents or other files that you need to move around with you. Larger files that exceed the 1.44MB limit can be placed on floppies through the use of *compression software* (applications that make data take up less room by packing it close together; common file formats include ZIP and ARC). Most back-up programs will allow you to use multiple sequential floppies to back up files, but there are certainly better options available among the magnetic media. Vendors still place software installation programs on one or more floppies, but CD-ROMs are becoming a more common medium for this (except for very small applications). Finally, floppies are prone to damage (such as temperature extremes and magnets) as they are extremely portable and sensitive.

Zip discs are one popular type of an option known as *removable storage*. The idea is simple: build a disc that can hold a lot more information than a floppy and use it for storage or as a movable hard drive. Zip discs are hard drives you can carry around and use on any workstation that has a corresponding drive that will accept them. They are a bit larger in size than floppies, but carry a huge increase in the amount of space (between 100 and 250MB for Zip discs, and up to 1GB for Jaz discs from Iomega, which makes both products). If an individual routinely works with large files such as image files, video, or PowerPoint presentations and needs to work on a number of different workstations (or even at home and at work), removable storage makes a lot of sense. It is also an easy way to back up a huge number of documents or other data files.

Magnetic tape is primarily an archival storage medium. Here, the magnetic material is not contained in a disclike item but in a format similar to that of an audiocassette. Magnetic tape can store a tremendous amount of data in a compact form—up to several gigabytes. The downside of magnetic tape is that information on the tape is inscribed sequentially, meaning that individual files are harder to locate. Individual applications cannot be run from magnetic tapes; rather, program files must be loaded on a hard drive in order to use the application. This medium is excellent for storing data for future use or for completing large back ups.

VIDEOCASSETTES

Videotape and the videocassettes found in libraries comprise another example of magnetic media. In existence since the late 1970s, videotape is currently the most popular medium for storing video footage and is only now starting to see challenges from DVDs and other forms of digital video stored in various computer formats. Videocassettes contain a reeled, linear tape that records and plays back video images and their accompanying sounds with good quality. They have been widely available in society for some time now and continue to rapidly grow in number. When coupled with the ability to record video using video cameras, the flexible attributes of this medium are likely to keep it popular for some time. For these reasons, libraries need to continue to provide videocassettes to their communities (when fitting) and, in many cases, be prepared to let patrons view them in house.

VIDEODISCS (LASERDISCS)

Videodiscs, also known as laserdiscs, were created in the late 1970s to contain high-quality audio and video. They resemble extremely large CDs or DVDs and use a similar laser-pitted track arrangement to hold their data; they also require a special player. They can contain up to two hours of high-quality audio and video (one hour per side of the disc) or up to 108,000 high-quality photographs and images. They have been used to distribute motion pictures, collections of images, and teaching tools. Videodiscs have appealed to educators because, unlike videocassettes, they can be easily used interactively for learning purposes. That is, you can jump around the material on a videodisc in much the same way you can on a CD-ROM or a floppy disc—choosing files or segments in the order you need them. Videocassettes are linear, and require you to fast forward or rewind the tape to get to the section you desire. Videodisc quality is much higher than that of videocassettes, but the amount of space on them has affected their popularity. It is not a good idea for libraries to begin collecting videodiscs, however, since not many people have players at home; likewise I do not recommend them for library use unless you already have them on hand.

AUDIOCASSETTES

Audiocassettes, dating from the late 1950s, have survived by complementing other audio technologies. They coexisted with records for many years and now do so with CDs. A magnetic medium, consisting of magnetic tape that advances between two reels in a plastic case, cassettes are relatively inexpensive to produce and can be formatted to carry between 60 and 270 minutes of sound. Their success as a medium means that many individuals in society have access to their playback equipment, which is often small, portable, and inexpensive. As such, they are popular in libraries for musical recordings, audio books, and foreign language study titles. They are easily damaged and have a relatively short lifespan, however, so they cannot be used for archival purposes. Cassettes seem to keep hanging on, although their linear arrangement makes it more difficult to find an audio track on them than on a CD.

E-BOOKS AND E-JOURNALS

The phenomenon of electronic books (e-books) is a new way of experiencing books. Digital versions of books can be created (both text and images) and distributed online as files or by using a storage medium such as CD-ROM or DVD-ROM. While many books that are no longer under copyright protection have been posted on the Web or elsewhere for years, e-books comprise a mixture of newer and older titles. Some companies who distribute them require specialized software to view them; the software may allow you to place bookmarks in an e-book, but it will likely limit your abilities to print or copy the e-book (due to copyright issues). Other vendors, such as netLibrary, allow you to download e-books to various handheld computer devices (such as Palm Pilots and Pocket PCs) or to your computer. All e-book publishers take care to protect their titles so they cannot be copied or printed out and shared illegally. It is hard to tell what this trend means for traditional book collections of libraries. It is likely that some titles may eventually only be published electronically and that libraries will need to find ways to contain and circulate them.

Electronic journals are already used extensively in libraries. The term "e-journals" can be used to describe a number of different items. There are electronic versions of printed journals that are made available on the Web by their publishers on a subscription basis (Academic Press' IDEAL at *www.idealibrary.com* is one example). Full-text articles from journals and magazines can be found in electronic periodical indexes (such as Bell and Howell's ProQuest, Gale Group's Expanded Academic ASAP [Infotrac], or EBSCO's EBSCOhost). Some journals, popularly called e-zines, are only published in digital format on the Web and may be free or available via subscription (see *http://gort.ucsd.edu/newjour/* for a directory of e-journals and newsletters compiled by people who post to the NewJour electronic discussion group). Libraries are becoming dependent on these electronic periodical sources, and their use will only grow as more titles become available. Publishers appear to be more and more willing to make their previously print-only content available online. The lure of publishing online only is also hard for creative individuals to resist (or those who wish to avoid the standard process of going through a publisher).

SCANNING TECHNOLOGY

There is one technology that is not a media format per se

but rather a method for placing information into various mediums. Computer scanners have been improving tremendously over the last several years and have grown less and less expensive. A computer only needs a scanner and scanning software to transfer physical items (such as periodical articles, photographs, and other items) into digital form. Optical character recognition (OCR) software, coupled with scanners, can also translate typewritten or printed copies of text into word processing documents that can be manipulated. Scanners differ in terms of their resolution (600 dots per inch—dpi—is a good minimum) and their color (24–30 bit color is acceptable). They come with one of a variety of different ways to connect to a computer, including parallel, USB, and SCSI connectors.

Libraries have been using scanners to produce digital versions of archival documents. Scanners have also assisted in adding images or documents into library Websites as part of the Web-design process. Another popular use is in the creation of electronic reserve collections for academic libraries, wherein articles from periodicals and other publications are scanned into electronic file formats and made accessible over the Web to students. The growing involvement of libraries in using scanners to create digital versions of information will impact on the eventual archiving of these materials. This interest is often aimed at preserving rare originals and making them available to remote users.

ARCHIVAL ISSUES

Libraries have an interest in storing information, both in its original format, if possible, and in another one, if

Figure 8–2	
Table of Archival Longevity of Different Media	
Storage Medium	**Lifespan**
Microfilm and microfiche	200 to 500 years
Books and paper	100 to 500 years
CDs, DVDs, videodiscs	10 to 100 years
Magnetic media (videotape, audiocassettes, floppy discs, hard drives, magnetic tapes)	10 to 100 years

needed. There are many decisions to make when considering how to store information for the future. A good spot to begin is with an idea of how long the format will last. Figure 8–2 lists the time period you can expect a format to last if it is kept under optimum conditions (see Jones, 1999 for more details): that documents or items remain untouched by human hands and in a room kept at 50 degrees Fahrenheit and 25 percent relative humidity).

No one expects that many materials will ever be kept at the optimum level of conditions. It is interesting, though, that the newer media formats are not predicted to last for anywhere near as long as the more traditional formats. What do the numbers in Figure 8-2 mean? Well, they should give libraries hope that some of the formats they have heavily invested in (paper and microformats) will be around for a while. They also make clear that in order to keep some media long term, a change of container or even a change of formats will be needed at some point down the road.

The conversion of images in a book (via a scanner) onto a Web page for display and then into a CD-ROM for archiving purposes or other use is already being done and will continue. The following six issues need to be evaluated when planning for archiving:

1. The hardware and software requirements for viewing or hearing a given format need to be considered before selecting one to archive items. It would be a shame to choose a format if its hardware or software were to become unavailable over time. This is almost unavoidable, however, and so archival collections often include not only the media but also the hardware and software that will be needed in the future.

2. Some thought needs to be given to the best format to keep or whether a new format should be chosen for a given item. Should you keep the eight-track tape of the Doobie Brothers, switch to a CD, or copy it over to a DVD? Many media allow for easy transfer to a new format for preservation purposes (such as copying the contents of floppy discs to a CD-ROM using a CD-RW drive). Others are more time consuming and have legal implications (such as scanning a book page-by-page).

3. Determine whether a highly controlled storage environment for archiving items can be provided by the library. This factor can affect what you archive and how long you can expect items to remain in good condition.

4. Consider maintaining multiple copies of items that should be archived. Place one in storage and circulate or use the other(s).

5. There is the question of whether materials in electronic format will remain in high enough use to even bother changing their storage format as time goes on. This is a question for all materials: Are they truly of interest to future generations and therefore worth

saving? If they are, you need to be thinking of the best ways to save them. This is already an issue for electronic formats, which are much less stable than paper.

6. If your nonelectronic formats continue to be used heavily, they may not last very long. Sometimes this can be solved by purchasing multiple copies, but this is not a financially sound plan for all items. How far do you let a useful item go in regular use before it is too damaged to preserve in another format?

Libraries need to seriously consider their archiving options and think about how important preservation is to their overall missions. With careful planning and continuing developments in archival technology, these decisions should grow easier over time.

DYING TECHNOLOGIES?

Just for fun, let me mention some technologies that are basically dead. New titles are rarely if ever distributed in these formats, and they have been superseded by current

---

Figure 8–3
Current Storage Formats Used for
Different Types of Media

Media	Storage Media
Text and still images	Books, periodicals, microformats
Computer files	CD-ROM, DVD-ROM, hard drives, floppy discs, Zip drives
Video	Videotape, DVD, videodiscs
Audio	Audiocassettes, CDs, DVD-Audio

technologies. Just looking at this list of technologies should serve as a sobering moment for those of us for whom these technologies were a lasting (or at least momentary) standard: records (LPs and 45s), filmstrips, 16mm film, eight-track tapes. What will join the list next? Figure 8–3 shows current types of media and the storage formats used to contain them.

SELECTED SOURCES FOR FURTHER INFORMATION

Breeding, Marshall. 1999. "Does the Web Spell Doom for CD and DVD?" *Computers in Libraries* (November/December): 70–75.

Crawford, Walt. 1999. "Up to Speed on DVD." *American Libraries* (September): 71–74.

Curtis, Donnelyn, Virginia Scheschy, and Adolfo Tarango. 2000. *Developing and Managing Electronic Journal Collections: A How-to-Do-It Manual for Librarians*. New York: Neal-Schuman.

Hawkins, Donald T. 2000. "Electronic Books: A Major Publishing Revolution (Part One: General Considerations and Issues)." *Online* (July/August): 14–28.

Jones, Virginia A. 1999. "How Long Will It Last? The Life Expectancy of Information Media." *OfficeSystems99* (December): 42–47.

Chapter 9

Adaptive and Assistive Technology

It is a good practice to make sure that technology be useful for all members of the library's community. Members of the library community who have disabilities may require an additional level of technology to enable their use of the library. The following pages explore some of the items a library may wish to add to ensure these needs are met. Keep in mind that this chapter addresses only the technology aspect; a library needs a comprehensive plan in order to truly serve this valuable part of our community.

TECHNOLOGY TO LEVEL THE FIELD

Assistive and adaptive technology makes the library and its resources work for users with disabilities. The terms "assistive" and "adaptive" refer to aids that either assist the user in accessing a library resource or adapt that resource in such a way that it becomes usable. Many of these technologies are aimed at adapting computer-based resources (such as screen magnification software and trackball controllers), but there are several technologies available for helping with more traditional library resources (for example, teletypewriters and recorded books). A careful assessment of the needs of those with disabilities in the community can help a library staff decide which of the following technologies are required. This assessment and the implemented technologies can help the library meet the requirements of the Americans with Disabilities Act (ADA). More important, it can ensure that the library is meeting its mission by providing all of its users with the information they need.

TECHNOLOGY FOR PUBLIC WORKSTATIONS

A standard library workstation such as the one described in chapter 3 is not immediately usable by patrons with some disabilities like blindness or limited motor ability. Fortunately, there are many technological products to make computer workstations easier to use for those with disabilities. Consider the following list a survey of products: A library may wish to focus its efforts on meeting certain accessibility needs that the staff have identified in the community; or the library may opt for a selection of adaptive technologies to cover many bases.

- *Screen magnifying software* is extremely helpful to patrons with low vision. These applications allow users to control both the level of magnification of the screen to fit their specific requirements and which area of the screen is to be magnified at any one time.

Figure 9–1
Screen Shot of ZoomText Xtra Screen-Magnifying Software

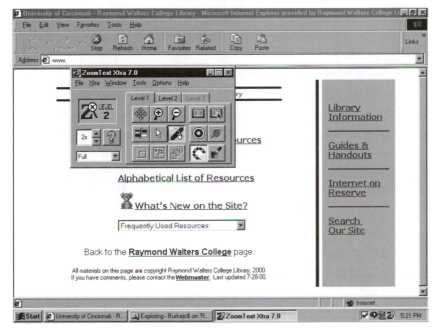

For example, users can magnify the entire screen at once and scroll through the entire, enlarged Web page or document using the mouse. Alternatively, users may select to magnify a defined area of the screen and they maneuver a boxlike frame around the screen to magnify each section (see Figure 9–1). Many other settings are available.

- *Screen reading software* extends the accessibility of any material one can display on a library workstation to those with no or extremely low vision. The software will "read aloud" whatever text appears on a library workstation screen, whether it is the library catalog or another resource. Users can choose from

Figure 9–2
Screen Shot of ZoomText Xtra in Screen-Reading Mode

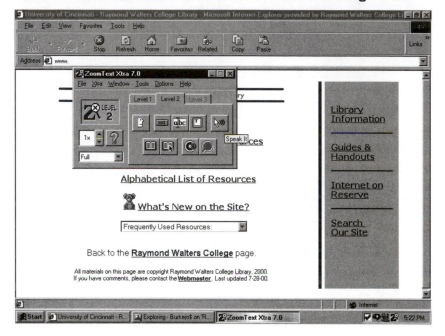

different voices, can adjust the speed of the reader, and can train the reader to skip certain unreadable characters or improve its pronunciation of other words (see Figure 9–2). Of course, any time a sound-producing device or software appears in a library, you should have headphones to accompany the software.

- *Touchpad or trackball controllers* are designed for patrons who are unable to use a standard mouse. Both trackballs and touchpads exert less pressure on an individual's hand, wrist, and arm. For those patrons with developmental disabilities or carpal tunnel injuries, these devices make workstation use more comfortable or even possible in some cases. Rotating a trackball with the palm of one's hand removes the need to grip a controller with the whole hand. Touchpads allow users to control a mouse by moving their index fingers along a pad that corresponds with the layout of the monitor screen.

- An *on-screen keyboard* helps patrons who cannot enter text using a keyboard. While most library resources do not require much text entry, there is still the issue of typing out search statements for the catalog, databases, and the Internet—even typing in URLs can be difficult or impossible for a user who cannot use the keyboard. This software makes a small keyboard appear on the screen that a user can click on to cause letters to appear in a Web browser or other application. This may be an excellent option for libraries, and can be preferable to the dictation software designed for word processing software.

TECHNOLOGIES FOR OTHER SERVICES AND MATERIALS

There are additional technologies that can make noncomputer resources and library services easier to use for people with disabilities.

- A *teletypewriter (TTY)* connection can offer patrons who have difficulty hearing a means for communicating with library staff members. A TTY device is connected to a telephone at a patron's home and to a telephone at the library (libraries will often set up

Figure 9–3
Screen Shot of On-Screen Keyboard

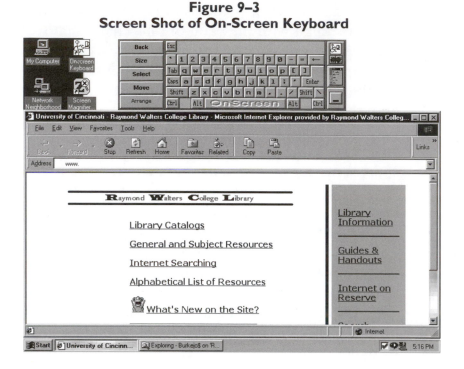

a separate line for this service). The device allows the patron and staff member to type messages back and forth. This can be extremely helpful for obtaining library information, asking and answering reference questions, and making other requests of library staff.

- Video-viewing station equipment should include the option of *closed-captioning* so that users with hearing difficulties can still enjoy the videos. Most televisions or television/VCR combinations include this as an option.

- *Book and periodical magnifiers* can make traditional library materials more usable for patrons with low vision. These units have a tray on which one can place a print publication. Over the tray is a magnifier unit that displays the publication on a screen. As with the workstation screen magnifier, a variety of setting adjustments are available.

- For patrons with extremely low or no vision, *recorded books* in various storage formats should be made available. Wonderful work is being done by dedicated talking book libraries throughout the world. This particular medium is an easy one to add to any library's collection. Most titles are available on audiocassette, but over time books and other publications are appearing in audio CD and DVD formats.

- *The Kurzweil Reader* in its many varieties has had a tremendous impact on making printed materials available to individuals with no vision. This device scans and audibly reads the information printed on a page.

- *Braille translators and printers* suit those patrons who prefer having Braille copies of printed materials. These devices require a workstation set up with translating software and with an accompanying printer that prints on paper with Braille characters. The equipment can be quite expensive, but not many libraries will need such a device.

WEB AND INTERFACE DESIGN CONSIDERATIONS

When approaching the design of a Website or a database interface, it is almost impossible to make everyone happy.

Without even getting into aesthetics, it is difficult to choose which features to include and how to make the site or interface easily navigable—plus, remember that there are individuals using our Website or databases who are not worried about the nifty images we may spread across our pages or the time we spend choosing color schemes. These are individuals with extremely low vision or no vision, who are accessing these electronic resources using screen-reader software.

One important factor is that there are a number of items (such as images) that are completely ignored by this reading software. Typically, people who use screen-reading software are also using a simplified, nongraphical Web browser. Web designers need to examine how their pages display in browsers such as Lynx. Images will not display, but image tags (like a caption) will appear in the HTML coding used to make Web pages. Designers need to make sure that important images that communicate information of some type also communicate that information through the image tags. This is but one facet that interface designers must look at.

There is some recent talk that Websites at community and public institutions (such as libraries) will eventually need to legally conform to site-design standards. The current prevailing standards are those set by the World Wide Web Consortium (W3C) as its Web Accessibility Initiative Web Content Accessibility Guidelines (often abbreviated as the W3C guidelines). The Sources section of this chapter lists some Websites that can give further advice on crafting workable sites and interfaces that meet the standards. It is never too early to consider what steps should be taken.

SUGGESTED LIST OF ADAPTIVE TECHNOLOGY FOR A LIBRARY WORKSTATION

1. the Smart Cat from Cirque Software—a touchpad controller (*www.cirque.com*)
2. Zoomtext Xtra 2.0—provides screen magnification and screen-reading capabilities (*www.aisquared.com/*)
3. On-Screen Keyboard from R. J. Cooper and Associates (*www.rjcooper.com/*)
4. pwWebSpeak—a screen-reading Web browser (*www.prodworks.com/issound/*)

SELECTED SOURCES FOR FURTHER INFORMATION

Center for Applied Special Technology. 2000. Available online at: *www.cast.org* [August 9].
Includes a variety of information on assistive technology and methods. Includes Bobby (*www.cast.org/bobby/*), a Web-page analysis tool that checks to see how well a page conforms to W3C guidelines.

DisabilityResources.org. 2000. *Disability Resources on the Internet*. Available online at: *www.disabilityresources. org* [August 9].
A directory of Websites on disability issues. Includes a section on making library electronic resources accessible to those with disabilities.

EASI (Equal Access to Software and Information). 2000. Available online at: *www.rit.edu/~easi/* [July 13].

Links to a variety of resources on adaptive technology. An excellent resource on how to make computers and computer applications available to those with disabilities.

Lubin, Jim. 2000. *disABILITY Information and Resources.* Available online at: *www.eskimo.com/~jlubin/disabled* [August 9].
A comprehensive listing of information and products relating to a wide variety of disabilities.

Mates, Barbara T. 2000. *Adaptive Technology for the Internet.* Chicago: ALA Editions.
Providing librarians with guidance on funding, choosing, purchasing, and using adaptive technologies.

New York Institute for Special Education. 2000. *Vendors Specializing in Technology for the Blind.* Available online at: *www.nyise.org/vendors.htm* [August 9].

Wright, Kieth C. 1995. "Technology." In *Information Services for People with Disabilities,* edited by Linda Lucas Walling and Marilyn M. Irwin. Westport, Conn.: Greenwood.
An overview of adaptive technology options for those with disabilities. Good coverage of TTY and related technologies.

Chapter 10

Technologies for Education and Instruction

There was a time in America when the public library was considered the "people's university." Today's libraries may have formal educational programs or may just occasionally instruct groups or individuals. Since almost all libraries have an educational function, however, an examination of instructional technologies is fitting. This chapter focuses on two areas of instruction where technologies have had a strong impact: distance learning and presentation technologies.

WHAT IS DISTANCE LEARNING AND WHAT ROLES DOES IT HOLD FOR LIBRARIES?

Distance learning is a method for connecting learners with educational materials. While most formal education takes place in a classroom, distance learning makes it possible for individuals to participate in a learning experience even if they are geographically distant from an instructor or are unable to meet in real time with a class. The idea is that a student can learn wherever they wish, whenever they wish, in an environment that requires independent work but is structured by an instructor and perhaps involves contact with other students. Several forms of distance learning (such as correspondence courses or televised and radio courses) have been practiced for many years, and all of them have involved one or more kinds of technology in order to facilitate exchanges and discussions between an instructor and students, since there needs to be some form of two-way communication available so that lessons can be sent out and feedback gained or questions answered.

Distance learning may occur at nearly any educational level, either in support of more traditional instruction or as the primary instructional means. Its growth as a method can increase opportunities for libraries to come into contact with it in one of the following three ways:

1. Libraries may support distance learning by providing resources for participants. This may involve making equipment available in house or providing information sources to help students with their studies. Academic libraries may need to support classes offered by their institutions through giving remote students access to their databases. Public libraries that offer Internet access to community users may find distance-learning students using it to download assignments or contact instructors. Libraries may also serve as sites for community groups to participate in videoconferencing. Whether our support is direct or on an ad-hoc basis, the implications of distance learning affects many libraries of all types.

2. Libraries that instruct their communities on how to use the library or its resources may well use distance-learning techniques to reach remote users or distance-learning participants. This would primarily apply to academic libraries, but other libraries may have opportunities to instruct remote users on an irregular basis.

3. Library staff members may themselves participate in continuing education or professional development opportunities via distance-learning technologies, perhaps taking part in graduate and associate degree programs in library and information science. There are also a number of other courses and workshops available to staff from other educational institutions or professional organizations.

Distance learning is not for everyone or for every situation. In each instance, a set of supporting resources must be available for the instruction to be successful. Sometimes those resources involve your library's collections so that you can help a distance-learning student find research materials for a paper or other assignment; other times the resources might involve equipment. Distance learning has the potential to be a liberating experience for students, freeing them from the limitations of the traditional classroom and class schedule. Since there are a number of situations where it does fit the need, we are bound to see an increasing number of opportunities becoming available.

SYNCHRONOUS AND ASYNCHRONOUS DISTANCE-LEARNING TECHNOLOGIES

Synchronous technologies are ones in which the instructor and students are involved in the learning process at the same time. Some possibilities for real-time communication and interaction include:

- *Radio* can be used to easily broadcast lessons to a wide audience at a relatively low cost (participants most likely already own radios). Students can interact with the instructor via telephone during the class if needed. The picture here is one of a lecture being sent out to waiting students who then complete assignments and send them in.
- An *audio teleconference* (like a conference call) can be used, and again is relatively inexpensive since participants are likely to have access to telephones. Follow-up interaction can also be accomplished over the phone if needed, as can video transmission (with some additional equipment—a process known as audiographics.)
- *Television* can broadcast a seminar or a class and can reach individuals in a local area cheaply and easily. Students probably own their own televisions, and so there is little equipment investment involved. Television becomes a more expensive option, however, if satellite or cable transmission is required to reach a wider audience. In these situations, it is more common to use television for brief (half-day) teleconferences that are sent to predetermined locations (such as schools or libraries) that can receive satellite or

cable transmissions. Interaction is again possible through telephone and, at times, e-mail.

- *Videoconferencing* is an excellent way to simulate the live classroom with its two-way video and interaction, enabling demonstrations of nearly any kind. It is rather expensive, however, because it requires videoconferencing equipment on both ends. It is not a practical medium for communicating to a large number of individuals at separate locations (at home, for instance), but it can be effective for focused connections between the instructor's location and a single remote videoconferencing classroom for brief workshops or full-length college classes.

- *The Internet* offers the possibility of a chat room or MOO (a Multiuser dimension, Object-Oriented) that can be set up for students and the instructor to type back and forth. A MOO consists of software that creates an environment in which several individuals can interact over the Internet. Here, the operational expense is minimal since there are many free venues online to set up chat rooms or use educational MOO space. Instructors and students can connect from all over the globe using their Internet accounts. The one downside is that the information transmitted is typically limited to text.

Asynchronous technologies are ones that allow delayed interaction between students and the instructor. In this mode, lessons are sent out and assignments and questions are sent back without any (or much) real-time interaction. Following are some examples:

- *Correspondence courses*, which are the time-tested method of distance learning, involve students reading a text or separate lessons and then taking tests to prove their knowledge. There may be a little interaction with an instructor to clarify points, but typically students work when and where they wish in order to meet course deadlines. Much book knowledge can be communicated in this way, but there is no ability to demonstrate processes or equipment in real time.

- *Video-based learning* sends videos of lectures and demonstrations to students, who watch them when they wish. It incorporates technology that students commonly own (VCRs and televisions) and adds interaction by phone or e-mail. Students have the freedom to watch the instructional material multiple times to help them review the material. However, as is common to other methods of distance learning, there are few opportunities for group discussion or interaction of any kind.

- *Web-based learning* is somewhat similar to these other methods in that learning materials are sent out and students can fit their use to their own schedules. Here, however, all course materials are placed on a Website. Audio, video, and static images can be added to text, and participants can interact via e-mail or Web message boards. The downsides of this method are that a level of computer literacy is required for students to take part, and that the equipment needed to produce and view the materials (as well as the knowledge base) can be expensive to obtain and use.

WHAT ARE PRESENTATION TECHNOLOGIES, AND HOW ARE THEY USED BY LIBRARIES?

Presentation technologies allow us to share information with an audience in a visual manner. Our presentations can be made more vivid and informative by bringing in visual aids through the use of display equipment, media items, and presentation software. While there are situations in which a verbal presentation will suffice, many times it is nice to either demonstrate an activity, to show the resources that are being discussed, or to illustrate key points of the talk in a visible manner. The methods discussed below can accomplish these purposes.

There are three basic roles for presentation technology in libraries: (1) the display equipment and media items can be managed and scheduled for use within the organization; (2) elements of the technology, particularly media items, may be circulated to the community at large; and (3) use of presentation technology can be incorporated into library instructional efforts. Both patron training in library resources or services and staff training in general can be aided by presentation technology, as can any informational presentation.

Display equipment allows a user to project text, graphics, video, or live demonstrations of electronic library resources onto a screen. While historically this equipment has included such venerable items as slide projectors and film and filmstrip projectors, today the primary means of display involve LCD (liquid crystal display) projectors or panels and overhead projectors. Overhead projectors are a traditional presentation tool that project either hand-drawn or mass-produced transparencies. LCD equipment can project output from computers, VCRs, television, and other items and tends to be expensive and require at least a somewhat darkened room to display well. An LCD projector is an independent device that can be ceiling mounted or mobile; an LCD panel sits on top of a high-powered overhead projector. Of the two, LCD projectors require less darkness to be easily seen, but LCD panels are somewhat cheaper, even when the cost of the overhead projector is included.

Computer presentation in all of its possibilities is overtaking traditional media items, but there are some individuals who prefer these older media, and some situations where they work quite well. Transparencies, typically massproduced collections, are sometimes found in libraries that serve an educational community, as are slides, which are easy to produce—virtually anyone can take pictures with slide film and have slides developed. Filmstrips may also be found in great numbers in some libraries, but they are very much a dying technology and exist only as very dated material. The more common forms of media used in presentations are again those that are in wide use in society: videocassettes, computer-produced presentations, and live views of computer resources.

Presentation software can bring together both old and new media to create a professional presentation. There are a variety of software choices out there. Three of the most common programs are Microsoft PowerPoint, Harvard Graphics, and Astound. Each individual screen or segment of a presentation is known as a "slide." Anything that can be produced or brought into a computer can be added to that slide: text, Internet hyperlinks, video clips, sound—you name it. The programs offer templates and preset designs for new users, but leave many creative options open for advanced users. It is not difficult to produce a professional presentation using this software.

SELECTED SOURCES FOR FURTHER INFORMATION

Heinich, Robert, et al. 1999. *Instructional Media and Technologies for Learning*. Upper Saddle River, N.J.: Merrill.
The definitive guide to understanding and using presentation and distance-learning technologies, along with a whole lot more. Good explanations of teaching methods and approaches for using technology for instruction.

World Lecture Hall. 2000. Available online at: *www.utexas.edu/world/lecture/index.html* [July 14].
Provides examples of Web-based distance-learning courses offered in a variety of subject areas.

Chapter 11

Troubleshooting Tips

Unfortunately, all of the technology we have discussed in the preceding chapters is prone to break down at some point. This can be a frustrating experience on many levels: We can't complete an action that is underway, as when a copier jams or our connection to a database is lost; or we lose our work completely, as when word processing software locks up and we can't save our document. Our frustration is compounded when we realize we are unable to fix the problem and need to wait for technical support.

If you spend much time using technology, however, you learn that many difficulties can be solved with a few basic skills. While I am by no means downplaying the importance of technical-support knowledge for an organization, I would like to suggest that many "fixes" can be handled by the end user, otherwise known as "you." The goal of this chapter is equip you to troubleshoot technology so that you will learn how to solve a number of problems on your own—and also know when to seek the help of experts.

TROUBLESHOOTING GUIDELINES: BE PREPARED

Preparation is a good prescription for any activity in the library—or in life. With troubleshooting, one of the best ways to prepare is to be ready to do some creative thinking. That way, if your preparations and methods fall through, you may still be able to reason your way through fixing a problem. Starting from that point, let's take a look at the preparations.

- *Gain and maintain common knowledge.* Treat each problem you encounter as a learning experience. There is great value in being able to remember an earlier solution to a problem you are having. It may not be possible to keep a written record of each troubleshooting situation and the solution to each problem, but it is crucial that two things happen: First, if you are involved in troubleshooting a technology problem, make sure that you see the final solution applied, even if it requires an outside expert; second, make sure that the solution is made known to all members of the library staff. This way, you can build up a group knowledge base and also empower other staff members so that they can possibly fix the situation if you are not available.
- *Be safe.* When you first approach a piece of malfunctioning equipment, remember the motto: first, do no harm—to yourself or the equipment. Safe practices come from knowing something about the item you are working on (for example, the paper can be removed from one section of the copier by lifting the

green lever and turning crank number two), and others are common knowledge (such as do not scuff your feet on the carpet and then touch the motherboard or you might destroy or disable it with static electricity). Avoiding static electricity and always reading any warning signs on the equipment are my best advice in this area. I have burned my hand on microfilm reader/printers enough times to make me more conscious of the marked "hot" areas. Another thing: these guidelines can help keep you safe, but I cannot guarantee that your hands will keep clean (any device that spews toner is bound to be messy). Get to know your equipment and do not be afraid of it. Read manuals and poke around. Work to get past any fears of breaking something; they can really hinder your troubleshooting efforts.

- *Check the obvious.* Some might reject this idea by asking, "How should I know what's obvious?" Here again, experience is our best guide. If you have a piece of equipment that breaks down on some regular basis (even months apart), you have a basis for obvious fixes: Look for the problem that happened last time and try to apply the same solution. Likewise, if you know something about how a piece of equipment works, you can check a variety of parts that are essential to keeping it running (is it plugged in, are the cables plugged in tightly, does it seem to be getting power, maybe there's a paper jam, is the projector bulb really working). When you face a problem with a piece of technology that has never broken down before or one whose operation is a mystery to you, it is time to turn to the next steps.

- *Look for clues.* Not to overstate the obvious here, but on occasion a piece of equipment or software will give off some clues as to why it had stopped working correctly. Sometimes these are very clear, as in the case of displayed error messages, and other times they can only be reached through inductive reasoning ("the paper only goes up to this point and then jams, so there must be something making it jam back in this section"). One technique I have found helpful is to have the patron or coworker who is having a problem with the technology explain to you how the problem began. You may be able to pick up a clue of what is really going wrong through some detail that the reporter provides.

- *Turn it on again.* The most successful troubleshooting technique I have found is a pretty easy one. If an electronic piece of equipment is not working, turn it off and then back on. The results are sometimes quite startling, and though you really do not learn anything about the problem from this solution, it is often extremely effective. I have had much success in using this strategy with computers, but I have also triumphed over errors with copiers, VCRs, and the occasional fan in the same way. There are problems with which this method will absolutely not work because it does not solve the problem (unfortunately, you cannot will a paper jam away or fix a machine that is already not able to be turned on) or it worsens the problem (for example, you will lose a word processing document in an application that has locked up while printing if you shut off the computer unless you saved the document before the problem occurred). I do recommend, however, that this technique be known by everyone in a library organization since it can be effective in so many situations.

- *Read the manual*. Though they are sometimes poorly written or too brief in their explanations, the manuals that accompany technology can assist in finding solutions or correctly identifying a given problem. While in the heat of the moment we are probably more likely to forge ahead without reading, it can really pay to take a moment and locate any manuals or help documentation you have. We hang onto these things for some reason, right? Well, this is the time to pull them off the shelf. Their diagrams can be helpful, and sometimes reading about the common problems that some manuals list can be educational ("Well, it's not that part or that problem at least. What else could it be?"). I admit that I have been frustrated by manuals that do not help at all, but I have also found solutions in others and thus vowed never to overlook this resource.

  A supplement or replacement to any printed material is the Web. Many vendors' Websites list troubleshooting tips or FAQs (lists of frequently asked questions) on solving problems, and there may be answers here that never made it into the manual. The same goes for reading the archives of a vendor-sponsored Web forum or a public Usenet newsgroup that discusses similar problems. Someone may have already located an answer and made it available to the world at large through the Internet.

- *Ask for advice*. There are some troubleshooting situations where we have truly reached a dead end and are unsure of where to turn next, and other times we wisely conclude that it is too dangerous to go further. Now is the time to seek advice from any and all quarters. Consulting the manual or the Web can be an example of this, but now it is time to try a more active approach. Post a message to a newsgroup, electronic discussion group, or vendor forum. Ask colleagues near and far if they have any ideas. Exhaust any technical support options that you have. I tend to try out my free options before incurring any charges, but your need for a solution may be such that you should go to the real experts right away.

- *Watch the expert at work and learn.* If you do get advice or direct assistance (in person or over the phone) that actually solves the problem, be sure to pay attention carefully and ask questions. This information can be really key to building up your experience and the general troubleshooting knowledge of the library. You may learn a new technique or discover that this really is a more difficult problem to diagnose than you thought. Be a student here and pay attention so that you can be better prepared down the road.

TIPS FOR AVOIDING PROBLEMS

The following are some thoughts on solving technical problems of one kind or another that have served me well over time. Your particular situation may not be covered here. However, one of these tips may help you in the future.

- Many problems involve paper jams or related difficulties. You should know (or learn) how paper feeds through all of the printing, copying, and faxing devices in your library.
- Printer memory errors are common when large documents are sent to older printers. Printers may lock up completely, or they may print pages full of characters and images. Know how to cancel print jobs and clear out your printer memory (it can be as easy as turning the printer off and then on). If you are in a networked printing environment, find out who has the power to cancel print jobs (if it is not you) and how to clear the entire print queue (the collection of waiting print jobs) if necessary.
- Dust can collect inside CPU cases and keyboards and cause them to stop working. A can of compressed air can be a crucial tool in these circumstances. You may wish to check regularly and clean equipment in this way. Computer mice will also pick up lint and dust and lose some sensitivity. Pop out the mouse ball every so often (look for directions on the bottom of your mouse) and shake out the foreign matter.
- If you notice even a minor problem with a piece of equipment that is used by multiple staff members or the public, be sure to note it to whoever else on staff might get a complaint about it. Forewarned can be forearmed in some cases; it is good to pay attention to smaller issues before they grow into larger ones. There are times when library staff may not realize just how often a small problem or error arises because no one remarks on it. We cannot force patrons to make note of problems, but staff can try to do their best to get the word out to each other.

- Put together a troubleshooting toolkit. This should
  at least be an actual toolkit, with the requisite screw-
  drivers, extra screws, cleaning equipment, and other
  items that fit your library. It can also extend to organizing your printed manuals and other help documentation, and having a list or set of bookmarks of
  where to go for more help online. I urge you to make
  this collection of tools available to as many staff
  members as are comfortable with troubleshooting.
  The initial collection of items may serve as a point
  to educate your coworkers (and become educated
  yourself) on what are some good troubleshooting
  strategies.

SELECTED SOURCES FOR FURTHER INFORMATION

Use library-related technology electronic discussion groups
(*www.wrlc.org/liblists/*) to ask questions of library colleagues.

Check the vendor's site to see if there are troubleshooting FAQs or user forums available. *Librarians Online
Warehouse (www.libsonline.com)* may be useful for tracking down a vendor's site, or you can use search engines
such as Yahoo! (*www.yahoo.com*).

Deja.com (http://deja.com/usenet/) is an excellent resource
for searching archived discussions for specific technologies and problems.

Dave's Guides (www.css.msu.edu/PC-Guide/) has a section
on troubleshooting computers that may be helpful.

Chapter 12

Protecting Technology

Information technology bears few dangers for its users, but users can be quite dangerous to technology. People can steal, damage, or even unintentionally ruin the technology we (and they) depend on. While it would be an overreaction to treat each patron like a suspect and to release guard dogs to roam among the stacks, there are steps we need to take to protect the technology we spend so much on. This chapter explores some of the areas of concern for security and some methods to consider.

Security measures are generally split between methods that attempt to secure equipment or media (such as cabling a CPU to a table) and those that attempt to secure software and electronic information resources. The first two categories below, physical security and restricted access, mainly deal with the former, while the last two, limiting functions and electronic security, handle the latter.

PHYSICAL SECURITY

Library security systems are very common at most types of libraries and provide physical security for materials in the collection, including some technology items. Most systems are composed of a set of sensor panels (with or without gates) at all entrances to and exits from the library. The sensors are set to detect an adhesive magnetic strip or sticker inside or on each item in the library. Items that are correctly checked out of the library at the circulation desk have either been "desensitized" (passed over a demagnetizing machine) or covered by a card and will not set off the alarm at the exit or gate. The systems are not without their flaws and failures, but they provide a sound level of protection for circulating and noncirculating books, media, periodicals, and other items in the library's collection.

For those technology items that need to be available to the public in house, there are a number of measures that can be taken to secure them. Equipment such as computers, VCRs, and televisions can be bolted or cabled to the furniture on which they sit. It is also a good idea to lock the case of a computer's CPU to protect internal components from theft. If a library has any items that are meant to be moved around within the building (such as TV/VCR carts, computers, film or LCD projectors, or CD players), these can be locked in a storage room to prevent unexpected mobility. Media items that circulate need to be tagged the same as printed materials for the library's security system. Items held in staff areas or that are easily observed from a service point probably do not require the same level of protection unless the overall security of the library's building is an issue. Be sure to perform an inventory of equipment or media on a regular basis to account for items and their security.

RESTRICTED ACCESS

Another way to secure materials and equipment is to restrict the public's access to them. This can take the form of having a closed collection of media items (for instance, placing all videos behind the circulation desk or another service point) or setting time limits on the use of in-house equipment (such as a half-hour on Internet workstations). You can also assign shorter circulation periods to certain types of items that you might consider to be at risk. Care needs to be taken here, however, so that undue restrictions do not hinder the public's use of technology. Seek a level of restriction that safeguards equipment but also gives the public ample freedom to browse collections or use equipment. Strict time limits or closed collections should only be applied when prior damage or conflict would dictate their use, or when they might deter attempts to elude security measures.

LIMITING FUNCTIONS

This method of protection involves restricting certain uses for technology rather than controlling access to it. While many types of equipment and media can have certain functions disabled by the vendor (a key lock on the paper tray drawer of a copier, videotapes that cannot be recorded over, microfilm reader/printers that will not make multiple copies of an image), the majority of solutions offered here relate to restricting computer workstations and software. There are a number of capabilities you would rather not let the general public have on your public workstations: deleting files, installing their own software, changing the look of the operating system or software applications. Some of these limitations can be implemented by using restrictions available in your operating system itself (options differ depending on whether you are using Windows 95, Windows NT, Mac OS9, and so on). Others will require workstation security software, which can lock up both individual software titles or parts of the operating system as needed. Most security applications have both preset options for shutting down a piece of software and the ability to restrict only certain functions.

The Internet has caused libraries to seek some ways to limit access to public workstations. Filtering software (see chapter 6) can eliminate access to a set list of Internet sites and be set up either on individual workstations or at the server level to control a large number of stations. An additional method of limiting Internet access is to install a *proxy server* to stand between library workstations and the outside Internet. While it can restrict sites, a proxy server can also limit the access of public workstations to certain electronic resources (and not provide full-blown Internet access). For instance, a library may decide that of their ten workstations, four should be exclusively for accessing their OPAC and periodical databases while the remaining six can be used to access the OPAC, periodical databases, and the Internet. The proxy server can be set to eliminate Web e-mail and chat sites as well.

ELECTRONIC SECURITY

Electronic security measures are primarily aimed at workstations and servers in the library. The issues libraries face with electronic security of their publicly accessible servers are similar to those faced by businesses and other organizations. The first issue involves protecting your server from people breaking into it and either damaging the server or using it for their own purposes. Library servers can contain all sorts of valuable data (OPAC records, library Website files, personal documents), none of which library staff would like to lose and some of which they would rather no one see (such as employee information and subscription sources). Libraries need to build a *firewall* between their server and the Internet so that these information sources maintain separate and secured access. A variety of software options are available to accomplish this.

The other issue in electronic security involves computer viruses, which are easily distributed over the Internet and by other means and can pose even a threat to libraries. Software that limits functions on public workstations aims to keep individuals from either downloading a virus from the Web or bringing a virus in on disc and running it on the computer's hard drive. Viruses tend to be more annoying than destructive, but having had to delete the contents of a hard drive in order to rid a workstation of a virus (and then reload everything), I can tell you that there is only a fine line between the two. Viruses can cause applications to malfunction and lock up, generating effects such as a line of text that automatically inserts itself in all of your word processing documents. Viruses can also reformat hard drives or surreptitiously corrupt important data files.

The two biggest areas of concern with viruses are: (1) patrons either accidentally or purposely placing a virus on a public workstation (as described above), or (2) staff members accidentally downloading a virus or receiving one as an e-mail attachment. E-mail attachment viruses are becoming more common and can easily be mistaken for a reputable file; if someone opens such an e-mail file, the virus goes to work. Antivirus software should be installed on both staff and public workstations so that the hard drives can be regularly scanned for viruses on boot up and downloaded files checked before they are run. Staff also need to know how to react when viruses are discovered on public workstations and to be aware of the dangers of viruses sent to their e-mail accounts.

A SAMPLE SECURED PUBLIC WORKSTATION

Following is one possible configuration of tools you can use and steps you can take to secure public workstations. Let's say you have one or more Pentium workstations running Windows 95 that are connected to a network and use the following applications: Internet Explorer, Adobe Acrobat Reader, Quicktime, a telnet application, a number of CD-ROM reference tools, and various other pieces of document viewing software (MS Word, etc.). You could use one, some, or all of the following products and practices for security:

1. *Set restrictions to the Windows 95 registry*. The Win-

dows operating system has a list of application settings called the registry. These settings influence Windows itself and any additional applications you might install. While you should be careful about making changes directly to the registry itself, you can use a free program from Microsoft called Poledit (or Policy Editor) to stop users from changing your settings on public workstations—such as the background image on the Windows desktop or the default printer.

2. *Use WINSelect software from Hyper Technologies (or a similar package).* This is an example of the workstation security software mentioned above that can be installed to limit the functions of applications on the workstation. For instance, you might wish to lock out certain functions of Internet Explorer (such as access to the MS Outlook e-mail program or the ability of users to set the default text size in the browser).

3. *Install, activate, and update an antivirus software package.* Two commonly used producers of these programs are McAfee and Norton.

4. *Set a CMOS password.* The CMOS is the semiconductor or chip that runs the computer. It has a small amount of memory in it which runs on battery power. This memory holds settings for the computer that a malevolent user could access and alter during the computer's boot-up process. Setting a password for CMOS access will restrict access to basic settings on the computer that, if changed, could allow an individual to bypass other security settings.

5. *Place the workstation in an area visible to the reference or circulation desks, and cable it to the furni-*

ture. The CPU case should be locked.

A SAMPLE SECURED VIDEO COLLECTION AND VIEWING STATION

If you have a collection of videos and equipment to view them on, this is one possible security set-up:

1. Shelve individual videos could be shelved behind a service desk (with a browsable catalog of titles available in a binder or as a subset of the OPAC).
2. Tag videos and their cases for the library security system.
3. Cable or bolt the VCR and television (or VCR/TV combo) to the furniture it sits on.
4. Require patrons to check out headphones in order to use the viewing station.
5. If there is a concern about damage to the videos, keep the check-out period fairly short.

SELECTED SOURCES FOR FURTHER INFORMATION

F-Secure Computer Virus Info Center. 2000. Available online at: *www.datafellows.com/virus-info/* [July 14].
A site that identifies computer viruses and offers solutions for removing them from your workstation.

Hyper Technologies, Inc. 2000. Available online at: *www.winselect.com/* [August 11].
The site for the vendor of the WINSelect security software and other security applications.

Public Access Computer Security for Windows 95/98. 2000. Available online at: *www.infopeople.org/Security/* [August 11].
A site that includes information on securing public workstations. Links to a variety of other sites that offer advice on security options, virus protection, and related topics.

"Public Access Measures." 2000. In *The Library Web Manager's Reference Center.* Available online at: *http:// sunsite.berkeley.edu/Web4Lib/RefCenter/lwmrcpublic. html* [July 14].
A section of the Web4Lib electronic discussion group archives that focuses on various methods used to secure public workstations. Lots of suggestions and product reviews.

Chapter 13

Building the Technology Environment

Just plug it in. That's all it takes to get going with our newest technological purchase, right? Find a chair and a table, maybe, or just stick it on your desk (or maybe over there on the floor). An outlet is all it takes, right? No problem!

Well, that all depends. Each of the technologies discussed in this book has a number of characteristics: how it is used, why it might be used, and so on. What has not been covered so far are some considerations about the ability of a given library building to accommodate a given technology. Some items will indeed simply plug in to a free outlet and work right away. Others will take more thought and preparation.

Beyond talking about issues of installing technology, there are also some questions about using the technologies. How can the process of using technology be made as comfortable as possible? These questions have implications both for staff members and library patrons, and are addressed below.

PHYSICAL CONSIDERATIONS

The library building needs to be considered as a technological environment. There are a number of characteristics about a given library that affect its ability to house individual technologies. Whether a library is starting fresh with a new building, redesigning existing space, or merely adding to that space, there are certain general criteria to examine. The determination of which are the most important characteristics will vary depending on the technology involved.

Electricity

Does the library have the electrical capacity to handle an ever-growing amount of electronic equipment? Libraries can find themselves either adding new electronic equipment to a building that has never had it or trying to place additional equipment in a nearly overloaded arrangement. Many pieces of equipment, such as computer workstations, can present a constant draw on electricity. There are a number of power-saving options available, however—such as operating-system settings in Windows or MacOS—that will automatically reduce processor speeds or set monitors to draw less power in periods of disuse.

Aside from overloading a library's circuitry, equipment needs to be protected by power surge protectors with a rating of at least UL1449. For servers or other equipment, *uninterruptible power sources* (UPS) may also be needed to eliminate the effects of unexpected power losses. These will protect equipment from experiencing the jarring effects of a sudden loss of power and will keep library systems and users from losing data. Library staff need to consult with electricians and computer support personnel to see what capabilities are available for electrical equipment and what protective measures should be undertaken.

Heating, Ventilation, and Air Conditioning

Can the ventilation and air conditioning systems of the library keep the technology within from overheating? In the old days of library automation, it was easy to stick the computer (or computers) in a single, air-conditioned room. Now that computers and other devices are everywhere in the library, thought needs to be given to keeping the heat down. Some equipment, such as a network server, should be treated as especially sensitive to fluctuations in temperature and kept in a separate, cool area; the general characteristics of a library, however, in terms of heat, cooling, and airflow can impact all equipment. Once again, library staff need to consult with experts in this area to determine optimum HVAC systems and settings to keep the library comfortable for people and technology alike.

Cabling and Connections

Can the library's current network cabling support new technology devices that are purchased? Or can the library building be rewired to support a new network? These are crucial questions in this age of networked information. Chapter 5 discussed networking options and raised the issue of library buildings that are difficult or expensive in which to add network cabling. In these circumstances, a library may decide to use a wireless network.

Just as with the electrical capabilities of the building, libraries must assess their abilities to offer access to electronic resources through computer networks. What networking capabilities are already in place, and how well are they handling the needs of the library? How will the library access the Internet (for example, via a dedicated T-1 line or by individual modems)? How many workstations will have access to a resource using the Internet or a LAN (that is, how many workstations will draw on a limited amount of connection speed through a dedicated line)? Is it possible to connect more workstations to a library's LAN (since demand for electronic resources will likely grow over time)? If an unrealistic assessment is made, the library will be unable to meet the level of access required by patrons and staff.

Lighting

The architecture of a given library will help dictate its lighting, design of which is crucial for any library and can have a positive impact on the use of library technology. Generally, lighting options should be chosen to meet the functional needs of an area of the library. Glare on staff or public workstations or microfilm reader/printers can be distracting and is a factor that should be taken into consideration when determining where to place equipment. Just as lights should be aligned over the aisles of the book stacks so that browsing patrons can easily see the titles and call numbers, lights over the public workstation area should be placed so as to minimize reflections on computer monitors. Where possible, staff work areas should include adjustable lighting to give staff members control over their personal workspace (as in adjustable lamps located at each desk or computer workstation so that light can be increased or reduced). Levar (2000) has some further useful information on lighting options.

Room and Layout

Technological devices are being engineered to be smaller and smaller in many cases, but they still take up space. When assigning room in a library to new technological devices or finding areas to shelve media, be careful not to underestimate the true size that items require. Though adding technology to a library may not always call for major architectural changes to the layout of the entire library, library staff members should be aware that there may be a need to reposition items to ensure a comfortable working environment and to let patrons easily navigate the library. In addition, when technology is placed in a library, visibility is key. It needs to be seen easily from staff service points so that staff can easily see when patrons need help. The guideline to follow is to place the technology in such a way that it does not impede traffic patterns or obscure its function (or that of another device, item, or service point), and so that it allows for easy access and use by patrons and staff.

Furniture

The furniture requirements of new technology have an impact on the room and layout issues discussed above. In many cases, the emphasis is on user comfort, for example, if dealing with computer workstations or media-viewing stations. In others, the question may simply be where should a new piece of technology sit. While it would be nice to always buy new furniture to accommodate new technology, it is more realistic for libraries to assess current furniture first. The important factor in all this is to consider the technology's furniture need before the technology is purchased so that suggestions can be sought from colleagues and vendors about the best way to fulfill the need.

A Checklist of Physical Environment Issues

The following list of six questions should be considered when adding any technology to a library (either whole new technological items or additional units of existing technology). They are not prescriptive recommendations (since all technologies differ), but they are starting points for you to use in discussions with vendors and those responsible for the maintenance of your facility.

1. Will the new technology have an impact on the electrical demands of the library?
2. Does the new technology require any special cooling or ventilation in order to operate efficiently? Will its addition change the heating and cooling balance of the library in some way?
3. Does the library have the necessary network or communications technology on hand to accommodate a new technology (be it a library automation system, a CD-ROM network, or a new full-text periodical database)? Will the current cabling system and Internet connection be able to handle this new item?

4. Are any lighting adjustments needed to make the use of this new technology more comfortable for users or staff? Is additional lighting needed, or should current lighting be altered to avoid glare or low-light conditions?

5. Will there be enough room in the library to accommodate the new technology? What may need to be moved in order to make it fit? Where is the most sensible place, based on its function, to put the new item(s)?

6. Will specialized furniture be needed to house the item(s) or make it available to users? Can current furniture be adapted to the purpose, or will a new purchase need to be made?

ERGONOMICS: THE HUMAN FACTOR

Does technology have an impact on those who use it? It certainly does. That impact can be a positive story of efficiency and freedom, or it can be a horror tale of eyestrain, muscle spasms, and migraine headaches. The latter possibility is very real, and as such necessitates a careful look at the ergonomics of the work and public-use environment with regard to technology.

Ergonomics is all about fitting an activity to a person. This primarily means making people's work situations as comfortable as possible for the tasks they must perform so that they can avoid injury. These injuries can be of the repetitive strain variety (also known as musculoskeletal disorders), such as carpal tunnel syndrome or tendinitis, or can involve other conditions related to vision and headaches. While ergonomics are clearly a concern for library staff members, patrons cannot be forgotten, as there will be some who spend extensive time working at a computer or reader/printer.

What steps can be taken to consider and positively impact the ergonomic effects of technologies in libraries?

- The furniture in staff work areas should fit the person who will be using it in terms of table height and location of the workstation. For furniture used by several individuals in public and staff areas, chairs and keyboard heights should be adjustable.
- Assistive technology should be used where it might help. Antiglare screens can be attached to computer monitors to help reduce eyestrain and headaches. Replace computer mice with trackballs to reduce the strain put on an individual's hand, wrist, and arm.
- Individuals should limit the time they spend on tasks that could cause repetitive stress injuries and take frequent breaks. Stretching exercises can help strengthen and relieve tension on muscles that might be affected. Individuals should remember to stop doing anything that causes pain.

Take a look at the ergonomics resources listed in the Selected Sources section at the end of this chapter for specific suggestions on implementing these recommendations in libraries.

THE VIRTUAL ENVIRONMENT: INTERFACE DESIGN

Now it is time to examine another area that libraries can work on to improve their users' experiences: interface design. Interface design is the art of creating the way people will interact and navigate electronic resources (such as an OPAC or a Website). Libraries subscribe to a large number of interfaces that we cannot alter or control (various public and staff-oriented electronic databases). It is therefore crucial that libraries take the opportunities they have to affect users' experiences with their services and resources. Libraries need to consider what they can do to make using their library even easier for their community. Some tips for improving interface design include:

- Resist the desire to tell users everything. Search screens and Websites can easily overwhelm people with information if careful design and restraint are not used. Library staff love to share information with their patrons, but be careful; keep the interface simple.
- Seek input from users on how to improve interfaces. The process of design involves lots of trial and error and can only succeed if users are asked to evaluate an interface along the way. It can sometimes be hard to get user feedback, but it's worth trying.
- Look at what others have done. There is value in being creative and inventive with interface design, but seeking out existing solutions can help the process. If an interface works or appeals in some way, the

principles of its design can either be applied directly to a new interface or can at least guide the new design.

SELECTED SOURCES FOR FURTHER INFORMATION

Currie, C. Lyn, Laurel Ritmiller, and Dan Robinson. 2000. "Taking Care of Ergonomics: One Library's Perspective." *Canadian Library Association*. Available online at: *http://209.217.90.93/top/cacul/occpaper13.htm* [August 11].
An excellent article that describes one library's process of assessing its ergonomics situation. Nice review of literature in the area and an excellent bibliography.

Failla, Victor A., and Thomas A. Birk. 1999. "Planning for Power." *American School & University* 71 (fall): 26–28.
An overview of electrical standards and issues for accommodating information technology equipment in educational facilities. Many items in the article apply to any technology environment.

International Business Machines. 2000. *Healthy Computing*. Available online at: *www.pc.ibm.com/ww/healthy computing/index.html* [July 14].
Information on ergonomics issues and improvements that one can make to a computing environment.

Levar, Linda. 2000. *Planning and Building Libraries.*

Available online at: *www.slais.ubc.ca/resources/architecture/index.html* [August 7].
A collection of links to vendors and projects relating to the construction and equipping of libraries.

Nielson, Jakob. 2000. *The Alertbox: Current Issues in Web Usability*. Available online at: *www.useit.com/alertbox/* [July 14].
A regularly posted column by a noted Web-design authority. Offers suggestions on solving Web-interface-design problems and gives tips on Web technologies to use and avoid when designing a site.

Trumble, Bruce. 1997. "Ergonomics and Design." In *Planning and Implementing Technical Services Workstations*, edited by Michael Kaplan. Chicago: American Library Association, 173–192.
Extensive discussion of ergonomic issues and solutions. Outlines a plan for assessing and addressing workplace ergonomics.

Chapter 14

Evaluating and Buying Technology

Libraries should determine their technology needs and also which general technology or technologies can best meet those needs. Once identified, the next step is to compare, choose, and purchase the equipment. With a dual focus of both evaluating the technologies or products and then buying them, libraries can successfully add the right technology at the right price.

ANALYZE NEEDS

The first consideration to make when adding technology is whether there is a need for it. The process of analyzing needs can be carried out in a variety of ways. Staff may have observed that there are too few public workstations available and that patrons are often milling about the reference area. Patrons may ask directly for an antiglare screen or a full-text periodical database. Reference staff may note that access to a collection of digital photographs and images would help students in a number of graphic design courses. Technical services staff may suggest that an additional printer—or bar-code reader or workstation—is needed to make the processing of library materials easier. If a particular technology suggestion would involve a large change in the library's services (such as adding a public scanner or starting an electronic reserve collection), then the groups who would be interested in or affected by the change should be surveyed. Perhaps the idea is just the interest of one person, or perhaps the need is stronger than initially realized. Whenever possible, build evidence that supports the need so that funding agencies and library administrations can have material to bolster budget requests.

LOCATE AND EVALUATE TECHNOLOGY CHOICES

Now it is time to search for solutions. Sometimes the solution is clear, but the individual manufacturer or model still needs to be decided. The methods and sources for seeking information and advice on technologies suggested in chapter 2 will prove helpful to locate the right technology or at least some possible choices. Consider the following nine criteria when comparing equipment, media, and electronic resources:

1. Is the technology suitable? Does it really meet the needs that have been identified? The needs analysis should have identified some problems to be solved. Now determine if a technology or product can provide the solution.

2. Is the technology close to obsolescence? Even if the technology meets the need, is there something better coming along? With all technology, we face the issue of it becoming obsolete as soon as it is released. This question generally forces us to choose between the new and growing technology and the old and widespread technology.

3. How durable is the technology? Can a copier stand up to heavy use? Can the database provider handle a large number of users accessing their service? Will DVD-ROMs survive the perils of circulating materials? Technology is expensive enough that it should be around long enough to justify its expense.

4. Does the technology fit into the library's environment? Is the item something that fits the mission of the library? Can a piece of equipment fit into the space of the library? Some technologies are neat to have but would not advance the mission or goals of the library. This is a checkpoint for assessing whether it is the role of the library to meet the need.

5. What implications does the technology have for training? Will it be difficult or easy to learn? Will bringing in this technology seriously affect training services? Sometimes the amount of training required can avert you from adding a particular technology right away.

6. What maintenance, upgrading, or updating needs does the technology have? Are these possible to complete within the library, or will they require outside assistance? Consider workflow—the requirements for staff to interact with the technology outside the information-seeking process. Also consider associated costs beyond purchase.

7. If the technology has problems, are there people available locally (within the library or its community) who can provide support? The technology may be easy to deal with, or it may require expertise. If the library has the expertise on hand, fine. If it does not, the library needs to decide whether it is worth acquiring the expertise, or if the expense of outside experts is acceptable.

8. How does the price of the technology compare with similar technologies? What will the total cost of this technology be (both initially and over time)? Its ability to fit the need should outweigh discussions of price (assuming the funding is there). However, there are sometimes acceptable alternatives to expensive technology.

9. Is this technology the most appropriate way to provide this information or service? Is there another format that would work better? Ultimately, the decision needs to be made whether the technology is really the most suitable choice. This final checkpoint should either eliminate nagging doubts or bring new ones to bear.

THE PURCHASING PROCESS

How purchasing actually flows in a library differs greatly depending on institutional requirements and processes. Many institutions structure purchasing depending on the amount of money you are spending. For instance, a $300 or less purchase requires the use of Form X, whereas purchases of $5,000 or more require Process Y (and attached

Form Z). Any substantial expense, such as buying a library automation system or choosing among companies from which to lease a dozen copiers, will involve a more formal process than buying individual media items. Decisions that have large, long-term financial implications, such as starting to purchase audio and video DVDs and the equipment to use them on, may well be handled only by the library staff, even though the funding agency will see increased demands in the library's materials budget for years to come.

The request for proposal (RFP) process is a common one used for those larger expenses mentioned above. A request is sent out to vendors who can supply the technological product or products that are desired. The RFP is a document that very carefully describes and spells out the criteria for the item(s) to be purchased. Vendors, if able to meet the criteria, respond to the library or its funding agency with a proposal outlining how they will provide what is requested. There is often a competitive-bidding process involved, which gives the contract for purchase to the lowest responsible bidder. At some point within the process, the library is able to evaluate the proposals or bids and decide which is the best one. If by chance the lowest bidder does not meet the criteria, the library can write a justification for selecting a higher bidder and have this decision approved by the funding agency. The RFP process can be very slow and sometimes quite frustrating if no bids exactly fit the criteria, but it is a means to evaluate a vendor and justify a decision.

BUYING GUIDES AND TIPS

When ready to purchase, it is vital to keep the following four practices in mind:

1. *Try before you buy.* Always find a way to look at and use a technology before implementing it in your library. It is great both to observe a demonstration version provided by the vendor and to see the same item in use at another library (if possible). Conferences with vendors' exhibits can be a great source for additional browsing and examination.

2. *Compare models and technologies with a vengeance.* It is far easier to just pick the first thing that works, but closely examining several options assures you will meet your need in the best way.

3. *Know when to stop looking and start buying.* As a counter to the last tip, be sure that you can control your comparison shopping so that you do not accidentally avoid fulfilling the need that got you started. There comes a point when you have looked far enough and can make a decision.

4. *Do not fall prey to myths about technology.* There are all sorts of myths out there, but here are a few of the most common: (1) wait before buying: technology will stabilize eventually; (2) wait before buying: prices for that item will fall before long; (3) wait before buying: that technology is about to become obsolete; (4) it's cheap and it's here: we'll figure out something to do with it. The first three myths assume that technology changes take place in a defined pattern. However, technology is always changing, and

if you follow these myths you will have to wait forever. The last ignores the hidden costs of any technology. The technology may be cheap, but it will
probably cost the library more in space, time, and
upkeep and will likely need to be replaced.

SELECTED SOURCES FOR FURTHER INFORMATION

Cohn, John M., Ann L. Kelsey, and Keith Michael Fiels.
1997. "Turning Your Specifications into a Request for
Vendor Proposals." In *Planning for Automation: A
How-to-Do-It Manual for Librarians*. 2d ed. New York:
Neal-Schuman, 55–65.
Outlines the RFP process and offers advice and forms
to use in your preparation of these documents.

Howden, Norman. 2000. *Buying and Maintaining Personal Computers: A How-to-Do-It Manual for Librarians*. New York: Neal-Schuman.
Excellent tips for purchasing computer hardware and
software. Good planning steps to take for buying any
technology items.

Integrated Library Systems Reports. 2000. *Sample RFPs*.
Available online at: *www.ilsr.com/sample.htm* [August
12].
Contains links to sites that provide guidance on writing
RFPs and that give examples of these documents.

Chapter 15

Writing a Technology Plan

A technology plan is sometimes looked at as a waste of time, or just a chance to dream a bit, put some ideas on paper, and then file them away. The plans that fit this definition come out of library organizations that create a plan and do not follow up on it, or that form a plan for one specific purpose and then abandon it. A technology plan, in my view, is not a static document. It is an attempt by a library to take inventory of its current technology, survey the needs of users and itself, and make a plan to acquire technologies to meet these needs.

Your technology plan needs to be a flexible document. It can be a very specific, short-term list of equipment that needs to be purchased to meet current service needs. It can be an inventory of current equipment that serves as the basis for a long-term replacement schedule. It can be a mixture of current and future needs, including both easily attainable and wish-list goals. Again, the plan is not something set in stone; it is more of an ongoing process to assess and meet needs. To do it right, a technology plan requires brainstorming.

There are many fine technology plans and planning processes to use as models when creating your own plan, but do not feel so tied to one that you ignore specific needs or characteristics of your organization. No two technology plans are alike—nor should they be—though on occasion, you may find that a particular funding agency will require a certain type of technology plan.

TECHNOLOGY PLANNING STEPS

How does a technology plan come together? The following seven steps provide an overview of the process and the key tasks to complete. There are a number of books and Websites that offer more detailed processes, and these are listed in the Selected Sources section that follows.

Step 1: Inventory Your Current Technology

Start by seeing what technology you already have. It may constitute a count of equipment or media types or both. This serves a number of purposes. First, you can get an idea of how up-to-date and functional your current technology is—you may realize from your inventory that you have a number of items that should be upgraded or replaced in the near future. Second, you may discover technologies that you did not realize you had (software, older media types, peripherals, and the like), and it may lead you to new uses for them. Third, you can refer to the inventory to check for gaps in your technology holdings that you had not recognized before. You may generally know what you have and what items are needed in your library, but when adding new technology you may overlook the cost-saving fact that you already own a part of the items you need. Replacement, reallocation, and recognition of gaps are all crucial benefits of an inventory.

Step 2: Conduct a Needs Assessment

Next, think about what needs you have that technology could meet. There are times when simply adding more of existing items (such as videotapes and computer workstations) will do the trick, and other times where entirely new approaches to technology must be taken. The only way to find out where you are and where you should be going is to take a hard look at your current situation. Be sure to ask your patrons—those using your library can give you some insight on what to add or alter.

This is a point where brainstorming should happen in earnest. Consider needs you may not have thought of before. As you assess your needs, keep an open mind. There will be a later stage where you will need to prioritize your needs and provide justifications for them, but your assessment at this stage can be based on both hard facts and on perceptions.

Step 3: Investigate Your Options and Opportunities

Once you have some new technology uses or whole new services in mind, you can turn to technology information sources to research your options (see chapter 2). This process should be focused on the ideas you formed in the previous step, but there is still room for new ideas and concepts in the mix. You may encounter a completely new solution to a need only when you start investigating the options available. Likewise, you may determine that you could follow another library's example and implement a new service you had not imagined.

Step 4: Set Priorities and Make Justifications

Now comes the time to hash out the importance of each change or addition you have established. Take the facts you have discovered during the last step and make the best case you can for each idea. Be sure also to note the drawbacks of each change. Then decide which ones have the most merit in terms of the immediacy of the need they will fill and in terms of your ability to bring them into being (both fiscally and operationally). This is also the point at which you can clearly articulate the benefits of the changes you are planning. Justifying the changes will help you decide priorities. With a clear list of changes organized by priority, you now have a sense of the timeline in which you can implement the technologies.

Step 5: Create a Budget

With so many technology changes, the deciding factor for when or whether something happens is money. Having organized your list of options by priority of need, now price them out. Consider all of the equipment or media costs involved, as well as the needed staff time to install the technology, train and be trained on it, and to handle any other incidental costs. Look ahead to what funding you can expect in the near future and whether there are additional funding sources to pursue. You may be in a situation where the only way to provide for your high priority items is to seek out grants. If, however, you do not have additional options, you can use the budget process to help finalize your timeline.

Step 6: Develop a Timeline

Once you have worked out the details, you should be ready to move ahead with your plan as funding and other resources allow. Now is the time to establish a timeline for the projects you would like to undertake. This can be rather straightforward, if your technology-planning process involves a single or a couple of short-term projects, or may mean juggling a large number of projects over, say, a ten-year period. Bring together your best guesses and estimates of when you can afford your changes and realistically implement them. Create a document that is specific enough to get started on immediate goals and projects (or ones that require a long lead time) and gives some guidance regarding all of your prioritized items. Keep in mind that you are writing a plan that can be altered as circumstances require and solidified as target dates near.

Step 7: Plan to Evaluate

One step that is needed before you actually purchase new technologies is setting up a plan to evaluate how successful the technology is once it is implemented. Is it accomplishing the goals you have set for it? Are your users actually using the technology? The idea here is to come up with some way of assessing the technology that will guide you in making adjustments to your current situation and in making future plans.

SELECTED SOURCES FOR FURTHER INFORMATION

The following list of resources should be of help when putting together a technology plan. Some of the links offer examples of technology plans that others have produced. The book by Cohn and associates (2000) has examples of plans from every type of library.

Cohn, John M., Ann L. Kelsey, and Keith Michael Fiels. 2000. *Writing and Updating Technology Plans: A Guidebook with Sample Policies on CD-ROM.* New York: Neal-Schuman.

Integrated Library Systems Reports. 2000. *Technology Plans.* Available online at: *www.ilsr.com/tech.htm* [July 14].

Mayo, Diane, and Sandra Nelson. 1999. *Wired for the Future: Developing Your Library Technology Plan.* Chicago: American Library Association.

Ryan, Joe. *Library Technology Plans by State.* 2000. Available online at: *http://web.syr.edu/~jryan/infopro/techplan.html* [July 14].

Wisconsin Department of Public Instruction. 2000. *Library Technology Planning: An Outline of the Process.* Available online at: *www.dpi.state.wi.us/dpi/dlcl/pld/planout.html* [July 14].

Chapter 16

The Future of Technology for Libraries

The future of libraries seems impossible to consider without talking about technology. As demonstrated in chapter 1, the history of libraries is a story of technology. When we think about the future of libraries, we need to approach the question much as we might approach the history of information technology. What technological developments in the world at large may impact libraries? What are libraries doing on their own that may affect their services and improve how they do business? Here are a view issues, trends, and predictions to provide a sense of what the future may hold.

NEW CHALLENGES

Some have suggested that as the Internet rises as an information source and communications mechanism, it may eventually replace libraries. It can easily be argued that the Internet lacks many of the information sources found in libraries and has no one to provide their services. However, as the Internet continues to grow in information and reaches a wider audience, how much longer will those objections be accurate? As bona fide information resources start to appear on the Internet as free services (*Encyclopaedia Britannica—www.britannica.com—*and the *Information Please Almanac—www.infoplease.com—* are but two examples) and as reference services expand, it is less clear what it is that libraries do that is distinct. Internet organizations or individuals could even take on the library's role of organizing information, and some would argue this is already happening with, for example, search tools. While I do not see the Internet replacing libraries or that it is already starting to, I do find it difficult to ignore these trends. We may well see libraries change into virtual, rather than physical, locations much more quickly than only recently could have been imagined.

PREDICTING THE FUTURE

Predictions are a lot of fun. We start with something we know well and then try to take logical steps to leap ahead into the future. What we end up with is at once magical and unrealistic and wonderful and perhaps horrible. As examples of this process, I offer two interesting predictions involving technology and libraries that were made more than a century apart. One has already been proven, while the other has between one and three decades to go before we can evaluate it.

The estimable Charles Ammi Cutter made a speech at the 1883 American Library Association Conference in Buffalo, New York (Cutter, 1883). The entire address recounted his imagined visit to the Buffalo Public Library one hundred years in the future, in 1983. In it, Cutter predicted devices similar to fax machines, a huge library collection, thermostats to control heat and ventilation, and a method for sharing card catalog information among worldwide libraries, all of which existed in 1983. Not so successfully, he imagined a library that employed a huge staff (including uniformed pages), had drastically cut the circulation of fiction titles (an evil of the day), and offered public readings of books via a "reading machine."

A modern prophet, Ray Kurzweil (inventor of the Kurzweil Reader and many other bits of technology) offered the following predictions in a recent book (Kurzweil, 1999). By 2009, Kurzweil sees wearable computers as common and inexpensive and most text being created by voice-recognition software. In another ten years, 2019, he states that paper books and documents will rarely be used; and that by 2029, visual and aural implants will allow humans to connect directly to a worldwide computer network that will put the Internet to shame. Sound crazy?

Here we see two different predictions at either end of their life spans. Cutter's vision of a future library shows that it is possible to predict general developments and even be dead on about some things that would have seemed outrageous at the time. However, he also had visions fitting of his time that show that it is difficult to entirely leave behind our present-day conceptions. The predictions we make can be trapped by our understandings of technology or processes and can keep us from making the right jumps to imagine completely new technology. Cutter wrote his speech after the invention of the telephone, and he was able to project that the telephone could carry data as well as voices. However, he had no context for imagining computers. Likewise, it is hard for us to imagine new processes that might be invented and implemented in the future, and so it is hard to even come close to predicting the changes that will take place.

Kurzweil's view of the near future needs to be treated with the same caution. His leaps are similar to those of Cutter in that they follow known technologies. Wireless computers are here now but not very widespread; wearable computers are being played with already; we can use voice recognition software; there are already documents produced in only electronic formats; there is a worldwide computer network. Kurzweil is taking the known and making it more common, and also letting some technology jump ahead much in the same way technology as a whole has jumped around and ahead during the twentieth century. Cutter's vision is familiar today, but we will have to wait and see if Kurzweil's will become so. As someone who plans to be gainfully employed in libraries beyond 2029, I am interested to see how close he comes.

TRENDS AND TECHNOLOGIES TO WATCH

Looking toward the future allows us to see what is happening right now and project what the future may hold. The following list of trends and issues involving technologies is not complete, but it is suggestive of what is happening now in libraries and where libraries are going. Some of the items on the list have been influenced by the Library and Information Technology Association's list of technology trends (Library and Information Technology Association, 2000) which are available from their Website.

1. Libraries' move to add electronic sources has created a tremendous reliance on them. As libraries devote more of their budget to electronic sources, they could see a serious decrease in their purchases of print and microformat resources.
2. The influx of many more electronic sources has made well-designed library Websites crucial to accessing them. If we cannot get our users to the resources we offer, we are wasting our money and their time.
3. Patrons still desire interaction with the human face of the library, its staff. Library staff members need to continue to find ways to aid individuals both in house and remotely while maintaining the high level of service our patrons expect.
4. E-books are growing more available. It will be interesting to see what impact this has on print publishing as a whole and whether libraries will begin purchasing these sources. The current link between e-books and various hand-held computers (such as Palm Pilots) means that libraries will need to pay attention to developments among these devices. Doing so will ensure that we can provide e-books in the formats that these devices can handle.
5. Full-text periodical indexes and electronic reference sources are growing in number and scope. What impact will this have on the collection-development decisions of libraries who now sometimes duplicate their holdings between print and electronic versions? Will patrons be so drawn to electronic full text that

they abandon printed periodicals? The answer to the second question is already "yes" at many libraries.

6. Computer hardware appears to be getting relatively less expensive while software is holding place or getting more expensive. This trend, if it holds, could allow more individuals to purchase computers and gain access to the Internet (for which the software and accounts are relatively inexpensive). Meanwhile, libraries may find the services of their automation system and database vendors growing more expensive.

7. Increasing bandwidth is allowing more data to be moved along the Internet and into individuals' homes. This could encourage even more people to access information from home, causing libraries increased concerns about remote patron authentication and the provision of digital reference services. It can also create fears that Internet searching will overtake libraries and their resources (which is not a completely bad idea).

8. Libraries are forming and joining consortiums and co-ops. This leads to increased access to informational resources for library patrons at a lower cost to their libraries. It can also lead to decreasingly unique collections of electronic resources, as libraries can only offer what is decided by the consortium.

9. Libraries and library staff need to stress their abilities to help patrons evaluate the information they find on the Internet and elsewhere. Patrons often have too many choices of information sources and need help comparing them.

10. Full-text sources of all kinds are affected both by copyright issues and the unwillingness of some pub-

lishers to make their sources available at reasonable prices (if at all). This might lead to e-books becoming more widely available. Were this to occur, the current fluid nature of full-text periodical and reference sources could be controlled, and libraries would not have to fear titles being pulled from a database by publishers.

THE COMPLEX LIBRARY

For the near future, we are likely to have what might be called a complex library: an amalgamation of various types of media and information sources. Traditional print and electronic sources will continue to be added to libraries, along with the need to integrate the use of these sources. As long as libraries can offer value-added services unlike those of other organizations or individuals, there will always be a place for our work. It is important that libraries stay rooted in their essential functions and societal expectations (books and access to information) while reaching toward amazing changes (such as truly virtual libraries that provide a wealth of resources over the Internet). The potential advancements and adaptations are incredibly exciting.

SELECTED SOURCES FOR FURTHER INFORMATION

Cutter, Charles Ammi. 1883. "The Buffalo Public Library in 1983." *Library Journal* 8 (September/October): 211–

17.

Kurzweil, Ray. 1999. *The Age of Spiritual Machines: When Computers Exceed Human Intelligence*. New York: Viking.

Library and Information Technology Association. 2000. *LITA Top Technology Trends*. Available online at: *www.lita.org/committee/toptech/mainpage.htm* [June 27].

Mann, Steve. 1999. "University of Toronto WearComp Linux Project." *Linux Journal* (February): 10–19.

An interesting investigation of wearable computers.

Glossary

56Kbps line—a leased telephone line used to connect to the Internet. Can transmit data at 56 kilobits per second (Kbps).

56Kbps modem—the current top transmission speed for modems: 56 kilobits per second (Kbps).

abstract—a brief summary of a periodical article. Often found in electronic periodical databases along with article citations and sometimes the full text of an article.

adaptive technology—technology used to adapt other technological equipment for use by people with disabilities. Somewhat synonymous with the term "assistive technology."

ADSL—see Asymmetric Digital Subscriber Line.

application—a general term for a piece of software or a program that can be used on a computer (for example, word processing applications or Internet applications).

assistive technology—any technology that can be used to help people with disabilities find and use the information they need. Somewhat synonymous with the term "adaptive technology."

Asymmetric Digital Subscriber Line (ADSL)—a method for connecting to the Internet over standard telephone lines that allows for transmission speeds of between 1.5 and 9 megabits per second (Mbps).

asynchronous—refers to technologies used for communication or instruction that do not work in real time (such as electronic mail or correspondence courses). Users of these items send out a message and then must wait for a response.

audiocassette—an audiovisual or media format for recording sound for playback. Consists of magnetic tape that advances between two reels in a plastic case.

audiovisual items (or audiovisuals)—items in a library collection that utilize sound or visual images or both. Examples include compact discs, videocassettes, and audiocassettes.

authentication—the process of ensuring that an individual has the right to use a database or other electronic resource.

automated search software—applications that will run preset searches on one or more databases or electronic resources. Can be configured to regularly run the same search to check for updated information on a topic.

bandwidth—a term referring to the capacity of a data transmission mechanism, such as a telephone line or a co-axial cable, to transmit data. The less bandwidth a mechanism has, the less data it can handle simultaneously and thus the slower it will upload and download text and images.

bibliographic utility—a company (such as OCLC) that makes a database of cataloging records in MARC format available to libraries at a subscription fee.

bit—simplest level of computer information. A bit can have the value of 0 or 1.

bits per second (bps)—common measurement of data transmission through modems or computer networks.

boot up—the starting process of a computer, in which the computer determines whether its components are in working order and starts its operating system running.

browser software—an Internet application that allows users to view Websites (for example, Internet Explorer and Netscape).

bulletin board—a method for communicating online in which messages are posted on a Web page to be read and replied to by others.

bus topology—a method for configuring a computer network that consists of a linear arrangement of workstations and devices in a roughly straight line.

byte—eight bits, which is enough memory to represent a single alphanumeric character.

cable modem—a device that uses the coaxial cable laid for cable television to provide users with Internet access speeds up to 2 megabits per second (Mbps).

card—a device that can be plugged into the central processing unit (CPU) of a computer to accomplish a particular function (for example, a sound card allows sounds to be played on the computer and heard through speakers). Other examples include video cards and modems.

card catalog—a paper-based method for organizing the materials owned by a library, invented in 1791 in France. Individual cards are filed for each item, and the cards are typically arranged by author, title, and subjects. Now being replaced by online catalogs.

CD—see compact disc.

CD-ROM—see compact disc–read-only memory.

CD-ROM drive—a device used to read the information or run an application stored on a CD-ROM disc.

CD-RW drive—a device that allows a user to place computer files on a blank CD-ROM disc and to write over them multiple times.

central processing unit (CPU)—the part of a computer that contains the main working components of the system, including the random access memory (RAM), the motherboard, and the computer's processor.

chat—a method for online communication in which individuals type messages back and forth to one another in a text-based, real-time exchange.

classification system—a method for organizing a library collection so that it can be browsed by subject. Examples include the Dewey Decimal Classification and the Library of Congress Classification Systems.

client/server—a computing concept in which a user's computer (the client) can make use of an application or resource based on another computer (the server). This concept underlies the workings of the Internet.

clock speed—a measurement of how quickly a computer processor works, measured in megahertz (MHz).

coaxial cable—a type of cable used to connect workstations and other devices in computer networks. Particularly good for transmitting large amounts of audio and video (as in cable television networks, which use coaxial cable).

collection control—the maintenance, organization, and growth of library collections using technological devices (in the context of this book).

collection development profile—a picture of the collection development needs of a given library (or part of a library) that can be configured in an electronic acquisitions system to shape the selection of materials through that system.

compact disc (CD)—a disc 5 1/2 inches in diameter and

that is used to hold up to seventy-four minutes of audio recordings.

compact disc–read-only memory (CD-ROM)—a disc 5 1/2 inches in diameter that can be laser pitted to hold up to 650MB of electronic information.

compression software—applications that make data consume less space; common file formats include ARC and ZIP.

consortium—a number of libraries that agree to work together to seek group pricing for electronic resources; may also participate in sharing their resources within the group. Just one term for this sort of cooperative arrangement among libraries.

copy cataloging—the process of creating a catalog record for a new item in the collection by taking an already produced MARC record for the item and modifying it as needed for local use. Unlike original cataloging, which involves creating a new record from scratch.

CPU—see central processing unit.

data—a descriptive term for information held in electronic format. Data may be a text document, an image file, a file written in a computer programming language, or an audio file (among other possibilities).

database—a method for electronically organizing information in a way that it can be easily searched and retrieved.

Databases consist of a collection of records, which are made up of a number of fields, each of which contains a piece of information.

database software—an application that allows you to create your own databases for a variety of purposes; one example is Microsoft Access.

desktop—the interface for the Windows operating system; through it, one can interact with applications using the mouse and keyboard.

dial-up connection—the method used to connect to an online catalog or the Internet using a modem to dial a phone number and connect to another modem at a library or an Internet service provider.

distance learning—a method of teaching and learning that makes it possible for individuals to participate in a learning experience even if they are geographically distant from an instructor or are unable to meet in real time with a class.

domain name—the alphabetic name given to an Internet site in place of its numerical Internet protocol address (for example, *www.yahoo.com* rather than 129.137.146.1).

DOS (Disk Operating System)—one of the first text-based computer operating systems.

dumb terminal—see terminal.

DVD—a disc that is 5 1/2 inches in diameter and that can be used to hold audio recordings (up to fifty hours per disc) and video (between two and eight hours of high-quality video). DVDs have much larger capacities than CDs or CD-ROMs and run much faster.

DVD-ROM—a disc that is 5 1/2 inches in diameter that can be laser pitted to hold between 4.7 and 17 gigabytes (GB) of computer data.

DVD-ROM drive—a device that, when installed in a computer workstation, can play either DVD-ROMs or CD-ROMs.

e-book (electronic book)—an electronic version of a book that may be read via the Web on a computer workstation or using a handheld device (such as a special reader or a Palm Pilot).

e-mail (electronic mail)—a form of communication that uses the Internet to send messages. It requires a user to maintain an e-mail account and electronic mail software.

electronic discussion group—an e-mail-based method for holding discussions with many other individuals on a topic of interest. Each message in the discussion is sent out as an e-mail message to each person who subscribes to the group.

electronic mail software—a software application that allows users to send electronic mail messages.

electronic reference source—a source of information in

electronic format (for example, Web-based periodical databases, CD-ROM encyclopedias) that can be used to meet users' reference information needs.

electronic resource—any information source found in electronic format. Can include electronic reference sources, Internet sites, e-books, and e-journals, among others.

electronic security—using software-based means for securing library workstations and servers to protect against viruses, hackers, and inadvertent errors.

ergonomics—the science of fitting an activity or work space to a person's needs to ensure comfort and productivity.

external storage device—a method for storing computer data in a medium that can be removed from the computer itself. Examples include floppy disc drives, CD-RW drives, and Zip drives.

FAQ—a document containing answers to frequently asked questions. Very common on the Internet as help guides to using a site or resource or as a source of detailed information on a topic.

fiber optic—a type of cable used in computer networks. Tends to be more expensive than other cabling options, but provides clear and quick transmission of data between workstations and servers. Used extensively in telephone networks.

field—a section of a record in a database that holds a specific type of information. For instance, in a MARC record for a book, there will be a field for the author's name.

file—a container of computer information that can be read or displayed by software applications (such as a word processing file, an HTML file, or a file that makes up part of an application).

file server—see network server.

filtering software—an application that is designed to restrict Internet users from viewing material that might be considered offensive.

firewall—a combination of software measures that restrict who can access information on a Web server or network server. Protects the server from being used or ruined by individuals who should not have access.

floppy disc—a 3.5-inch square disc that can be used to store computer data externally. The disc can be removed from the computer and stored elsewhere or used to transport data from place to place. It has a capacity of 1.44 megabytes (MB).

floppy drive—a device that stores data on a floppy disc.

full text—a term that describes the provision of the entire text of a periodical article or other source. An item called "full text" should contain everything in it that appeared in a printed version (or other original format).

full-text reference source—electronic reference sources such as encyclopedias, handbooks, and biographical sources that may be Web based or available on CD-ROM. The electronic reference source repeats the text information of the original printed source.

gateways—devices used in wide area networks that translate between local area networks that use different communication protocols.

gigabyte (GB)—one billion bytes; common measurement of hard drive and storage space.

gopher sites—Internet sites that are accessed using gopher protocol, an older method for arranging and displaying information online. Now superseded by the World Wide Web.

graphical user interface (GUI)—a computer interface that allows you to interact with applications, Internet sites, and other items by "clicking" a computer mouse to select graphical icons on your computer monitor.

hard drive—an internal-storage device for a computer workstation. Has the capacity to hold many different software programs and files. Current hard drive sizes are typically measured in gigabytes.

hardware—the physical devices that make up or can be used with a computer workstation (such as CPU, monitor, keyboard, printer, and scanner).

host computer—another way to describe a network server, which holds and serves, or hosts, a database or application of some kind. For instance, in order to run a library automation system, the library needs a server to host the system so that users can access it.

HTML—see hypertext markup language.

hyperlink—the ability to construct a word or image on a Web page that a user can click on to be linked to another Website or document.

hypertext document—a Web document created using hypertext markup language (HTML).

hypertext markup language (HTML)—a series of tagged commands that can be used to construct a Web document. HTML controls the formatting and interactivity of Web pages with other files on the Web (such as audio, video, images.

icon—a small graphical image used in computer operating systems and on the Web as a link to applications or documents.

image tag—in HTML documents, an element that controls how an image is displayed.

information technology—any items or methods for containing, transmitting, and storing information.

input device—used to enter information into a computer (such as a keyboard or mouse).

integrated online library system (IOLS)—see library automation system.

interface—the place in which the user interacts with a computer operating system, a library database, or anything else created or accessed using a computer. The interface displays on the screen as an application is used and controls how the user influences the application through keyboard or mouse commands.

internal storage device—a device that stores computer data; it is located within the computer's central processing unit.

Internet—the "network of all networks"; a worldwide computer network (developed in 1969) that has revolutionized communications and information exchange.

Internet access—the means by which an individual connects to the Internet to use its services.

Internet protocol (IP)—a system for naming Internet servers to make it easy for individuals to connect to network servers located anywhere in the world. Each server on the Internet has its own numerical IP number, or address (for example, 209.34.122.4).

Internet service provider (ISP)—a company that provides Internet access to individuals or organizations for a fee.

Internet-based resource—an information source or reference database that sits on the Internet and requires Internet access to use it.

intranet—a network that has limited its access to the members of a particular company or organization.

intranet-based resource—an information source or database that sits on an internal network, which controls its access.

IP address—see Internet protocol.

ISBN (International Standard Book Number)—assigned to each book as an identifier. Often a searchable field in library automation systems and acquisitions systems.

ISDN (Integrated Service Digital Network)—a method for connecting to the Internet that uses standard telephone lines to provide access speeds up to 128Kbps.

ISP—see Internet service provider.

ISSN (International Standard Serial Number)—assigned to each periodical as an identifier. Often a searchable field in library automation systems and bibliographic databases.

keyword—a term that can be used to search a database or Internet search engine.

keyword searching—gives users the flexibility to search all the information in a bibliographic record or a full text periodical article to retrieve items that hold the keyword.

kilobyte (K)—one thousand bytes; equivalent to a short note on a single sheet of paper.

LAN—see local area network,

LCD panel—display equipment that allows a user to project text, graphics, video, or live demonstrations of electronic library resources onto a screen. The panel sits on top of an overhead projector to accomplish this purpose.

LCD projector—display equipment that allows a user to project text, graphics, video, or live demonstrations of electronic library resources onto a screen. Contains its own projector.

library automation system—a product that computerizes a variety of library functions including the public catalog, circulation, cataloging, acquisitions, and serials.

Linux—a free computer operating system developed with networking in mind.

local area network (LAN)—a network that extends over a relatively small geographical area. Can involve anywhere from two to several dozen workstations connected to a network server.

log-in ID—the user name and password required to allow an individual access to a network.

Lynx—a text-based browser commonly used by individuals with visual disabilities.

machine-readable cataloging (MARC) record—an electronic record containing a number of fields full of information about an item in an online catalog (books, videos, Internet resources, and so on).

Macintosh—a computer developed in the early 1980s by the Apple Corporation. The first computer to popularize a graphical user interface (GUI) and the use of a computer mouse.

MacOS—the operating system for Macintosh computers.

magnetic media—storage devices created by using electrical impulses to inscribe information in a certain pattern on magnetic material. Examples include hard drives, floppy discs, Zip discs, magnetic tape, videocassettes, and audiocassettes.

magnetic tape—a form of magnetic media primarily used for the archival storage of computer data. Looks a lot like an audiocassette.

mainframe—a powerful computer that has been used in the past to host library automation systems and other applications. Now mostly superseded by smaller network servers.

management software—applications that assist with the operation of libraries and other organizations. Examples include a variety of office software tools that provide word processing, spreadsheet, and database capabilities.

MARC—see machine-readable cataloging record.

media items—see audiovisual items.

megabyte (MB)—one million bytes; equivalent to 200–300 pages of text.

megahertz (MHz)—common measurement of the internal speed of a computer's processor.

meta-search software—a type of application that can be installed on a computer with Internet access or a network server so that a user can search a variety of information sources at the same time. For instance, a library may wish to offer combined searches of their online catalog and their periodical databases from a single search blank.

microfiche—a medium used to store miniaturized images of pages of text or diagrams on a small sheet of photographic film. A standard microfiche sheet can hold between sixty and ninety-eight pages.

microfilm—a medium used to store miniaturized images of pages of text or diagrams on a roll of photographic film. Microfilm can accommodate between 1,000 and 1,500 pages per 100-foot roll of 32mm film.

microformat—a term used to refer to microfiche and microfilm together.

modem—a device that translates the data a computer is sending into a format, or protocol, that can be sent through standard telephone lines at speeds up to 56 kilobits per second (Kbps). Allows anyone with a computer, a modem, and a telephone line to gain access to the resources on a network.

module—a software program that handles a specific function within a library automation system (such as a circulation module).

monitor—a device that provides visual display of computer applications.

MOO—see multiuser dimension, object-oriented.

motherboard—a piece of circuitry that serves as the foundation for the workings of a computer.

mouse—a computer-input device that controls applications through the movement of an arrow in a graphical user interface.

multifunction system—a library automation system that offers more than one module in the same package.

multiple user access—the ability for more than one user to access an electronic library resource at one time.

multitasking—the ability of a computer operating system to have multiple applications running at the same time and to allow users to switch back and forth between them.

multiuser dimension, object-oriented (MOO)—software used to create an environment in which several individuals can interact over the Internet.

network—a method for sharing applications or information between two or more workstations. Very common in the library world for sharing information resources.

network cabling—the cables that are used to connect the components of a network. Common cable types include unshielded twisted pair, coaxial, and fiber optic.

network interface card—a card that plugs into the motherboard of a computer so that it can communicate with other computers through a network.

network operating system—software used to manage access and operations in a network.

network server—a computer that is configured to offer applications, files, or other reources to the workstations connected to a network.

network topology—the arrangement of servers, workstations, and other devices in a network. Common network topologies include bus, ring, and star.

Novell Netware—a common network operating system.

on-screen keyboard—a keyboard interface that displays on the computer screen and can be used by clicking on its keys with a mouse in order to enter text. Helpful for those individuals with physical disabilities that constrain their abilities to type with a standard keyboard.

online catalog (OPAC)—see online public access catalog.

online pathfinder—a Web document that contains lists of electronic and print resources that are useful for research in a particular topic area. The electronic resources can be directly linked to and from the pathfinder.

online public access catalog (OPAC)—the computer version of the card catalog. Allows an individual to search the holdings of a library through an electronic interface.

online searching—the ability to search electronic versions of periodical indexes and other reference resources through a dial-up connection or the Internet.

OPAC—see online public access catalog.

operating system—the environment in which all other software operates in a computer (for example, Microsoft Windows and MacOS).

optical character recognition (OCR)—using software to scan typewritten or printed copies of text and then turn them into word processing documents that can be manipulated.

original cataloging—a process in which a skilled cataloger examines an item and enters author, title, and publication information, as well as meaningful subject headings, into a cataloging system to create a MARC record for display in the online catalog.

parallel—one method for connecting scanners and other devices to a computer workstation, in this case using a parallel port on the central processing unit.

PC—see personal computer.

periodical—a publication that appears on some regular basis (such as magazines, journals, newspapers).

periodical database—an electronic version of a periodical index. Can contain article citations, abstracts, and full text.

periodical index—began as a printed reference source that allows a user to search for periodical article citations alphabetically by subject (or perhaps by author or title as well). Now available in electronic format as periodical databases with added searching features and, in some cases, the full text of an article linked to its citation.

peripheral—one of a variety of computer hardware items that have specific functions or capabilities (for example, printers and scanners).

personal computer (PC)—a computer workstation that includes a central processing unit, a monitor, a keyboard, and a mouse.

physical security—security measures put in place for the purpose of keeping library technology materials from being removed from the library; includes cabling or bolting equipment to work area furniture, and utilizing a library security system to tag media items.

presentation software—computer software that allows a presenter to organize a collection of information and media into a professional presentation.

presentation technology—allows information to be shared with an audience in a visual manner using display equipment, media items, and presentation software.

printer—a computer peripheral that produces paper copies of information that have been displayed in a computer application.

processor—a device that powers the calculations a computer must make to run software and process information. Located inside the central processing unit attached to the motherboard. Common processors include the Pentium line for PCs and PowerPCs for Macs.

program—see software.

protocol—a format for communicating data through a network or between different networks (for example, Internet protocol).

proxy server—a device that stands between public workstations and the Internet. It can be used to allow those workstations to seamlessly connect to subscription databases or to restrict the workstations to access only preselected Internet sites.

RAM—see random access memory.

random access memory (RAM)—memory cards that plug into a computer motherboard to give software temporary space to use while it is running. Generally, the more RAM a computer has, the faster it can operate.

real-time communication—communication that happens on a synchronous basis, similar to an in-person conversation (that is, one person speaks and is heard by another person at the same time, then the two switch roles; there is no gap or loss of time in their interchange as there can be in Internet communications).

recon—the process of converting catalog cards to MARC records for each item in a library's collection when it moves to an online catalog.

record—a segment of a computer database that represents all the information on, say, one book or one article. The information within a record is broken down into individual fields, which are typically searchable in online catalogs or periodical databases.

remote access—the ability for users to connect to data resources (such as Websites, online catalogs, and periodical databases) from distant locations.

remote information services—a corporate term for remotely accessed information sources such as Internet-based resources and those reached through the process of online searching.

removable storage—devices that allow for the storing of computer data on media that can be removed from the central processing unit (such as floppy drives and discs, Zip drives and discs, CD-R drives and CD-ROMs).

request for proposal (RFP)—a process in which vendors

respond to a written-out set of criteria for a needed product or service with detailed proposals of how they will meet the criteria. Typically used with technology purchases that involve large amounts of money.

ring topology—a method for configuring a computer network that consists of workstations and devices connected by a long loop of cable.

routers—devices that help exchange information between separate networks that are combined in a wide area network (for example, the Internet).

scanner—a computer peripheral device that copies physical items (such as periodical articles and photographs) into digital form. The process requires that the device be connected to a computer and that the computer have scanning software installed on it.

screen-reading software—software that will read aloud whatever text appears on a workstation screen when the software is installed and run on a workstation. In this way, any material one can display on a workstation screen can be accessible to those with no or extremely low vision.

SCSI—one method for connecting scanners and other devices to a computer workstation, in this case using a SCSI connector on the central processing unit. SCSI stands for Small Computer System Interface and is pronounced "scuzzy."

server—general term for a computer that makes files, applications, or Websites available to users of a network or the World Wide Web. See also network server and Web server.

slide—(1) an individual screen or segment of a presentation created using presentation software; (2) an audiovisual format of small pieces of photographic film that can be projected on a screen (on the wane as an item found in library collections).

software—programs or applications that make the computer do what the user wants it to do. Examples include operating systems, word processors, and Internet browsers.

sound card—a device that enables a computer to play sounds through speakers or to record them through a microphone. It plugs into the motherboard of the computer inside the central processing unit.

source aggregator—a term describing electronic library resource vendors that provide access to a large number of different information sources (such as periodical databases and full-text reference sources).

spreadsheet software—a computer application used to compile budget and other statistical information in spreadsheet form.

stand-alone system—a library automation system that only uses a single module or a combination of nonintegrated modules that do not share data; could consist of a system that has just a cataloging module, or one that has a circulation module that does not automatically update the OPAC module when a book is checked out.

star topology—a method for configuring a computer network with a central hub or server with workstations and devices reaching out from the hub on separate strands of cable.

synchronous—refers to technologies used for communication or instruction that work in real time (for example, chat or videoconferencing). Users of these items are able to hold conversations as if they were talking in person.

T-1—a leased telephone line that can transmit data at 1.544 megabits per second (Mbps). Used by organizations that require high-speed connections to the Internet.

T-3—a leased telephone line that can transmit data at 43 megabits per second (Mbps). These lines form the backbone of the Internet, quickly transmitting e-mail messages, files, and requests to view Web pages from an individual's computer to another computer or server.

tape drive—device used to save computer files on magnetic tape cassettes for archival storage.

technical support—the help provided by vendors for their products. Technical support may be available at no charge for those who have purchased a product, or it may be fee based. It is usually only available by telephone.

technology—a practical or industrial art that involves both products and processes invented by people.

technology plan—an attempt by a library to take inventory of their current technology, survey the needs of their users and themselves, and make a plan to acquire technologies to meet these needs.

teletypewriter (TTY)—a device that users who have difficulty hearing can use to type messages back and forth with a library staff member in order to access library information.

terminal—a device resembling a computer monitor with a keyboard that accessed applications placed on a mainframe computer.

text based—refers to an application (such as a database or library automation system) that does not make use of a graphical user interface (GUI) but rather relies on text commands that are typed in.

touchpad—a computer-input device that fulfills the functions of a mouse by having the user touch a flat pad to move an arrow on the screen.

trackball controller—a computer-input device that fulfills the functions of a mouse by having the user move a ball with his or her palm to move an arrow on the screen.

troubleshooting—the act of investigating and solving technical problems with computer equipment, software applications, and other devices.

turnkey—a product (such as a local area network or a library automation system) provided by a vendor that includes all the necessary components so that all a library needs to do to start using it is to "turn the key" (that is, press the power button). In this situation, the product is also typically assembled on site by the vendor.

uniform resource locator (URL)—the address of a Website (or other Internet resource); for the Web, it takes the form of http:// followed by the domain name and specific location of the site's files.

UNIX—a computer operating system initially used only on mainframes that is now widely used for large-scale networking purposes and on the Internet. Tends to appear only on network servers and not on individual workstations.

unshielded twisted pair (UTP)—a type of cable used in computer networks. Used extensively for data transmission in libraries and educational institutions.

URL—see uniform resource locator.

USB—a method for connecting peripheral computer devices to a central processing unit. It stands for Universal Serial Bus, and is now widely used because it provides high-speed communications between devices and the CPU, and because it is easy to add many devices to the same USB port on the CPU.

Usenet—an asynchronous method of communications on the Internet that consists of posting questions, announcements, or replies to messages in a topical newsgroup. Thousands of newsgroups are accessible using a Web browser or a separate newsreader application.

vendor—a producer or seller of a product.

vendor-based resource—an electronic resource that is accessed directly from a vendor's server. This requires subscribing libraries to use whatever method of authentication the vendor requires in order to allow access to their patrons.

video card—a device that enables a computer to display images on its monitor that are generated by applications. It plugs into the motherboard of the computer inside the central processing unit.

videocassette—an audiovisual or media format for recording video and sound for playback. Consists of a reeled, linear tape in a rectangular plastic case. It is currently the most popular means for sharing and viewing video and is widely available in libraries.

videodisc—an audiovisual or media format for recording video and sound for playback. Consists of a large disc (like an oversized CD or DVD) that can contain up to two hours of high-quality audio or video. Videodiscs are on their way out as a technology with the steady popularity of video-cassettes and the emergence of DVD. Also known as laserdiscs.

virus—maliciously written computer applications. Once downloaded and run on an individual's computer, they can cause applications to malfunction and lock up. In extreme cases, they can be designed to reformat hard drives or surreptitiously to corrupt important data files.

WAN—see wide area network.

Web server—a network server that hosts a Website.

wide area network (WAN)—a network that connects multiple local area networks (for example, a network at a branch library with a network at the main library).

Windows—the computer operating system used for most PC workstations.

Windows NT—an operating system for PCs that was developed with networking computers in mind.

wireless network—a network in which radio signal and infrared transmission technologies allow computers to communicate with other workstations and network servers.

word processing software—applications used for preparing memos, handouts, and other documents.

workstation—see personal computer.

Z39.50—an international standard for electronic information resources that allows compatible resources to be searched from a single interface.

Zip disc—a square disc (just slightly larger than a floppy disc) that can be used to externally store computer data. The disc can be removed from the computer and stored elsewhere or used to transport data from place to place. It has a capacity of 100 or 250 megabytes (MB).

Zip drive—a device that is used to store data on a Zip disc.

Index

About The Author

John J. Burke holds the rank of Associate Librarian and the title of Systems/Public Services Librarian at Raymond Walters College, a branch campus of the University of Cincinnati in Blue Ash, Ohio. Aside from his duties within the library, he serves as program advisor and teaches courses in the college's Library Technology associate degree program, which offers continuing education opportunities to library support-staff members. He holds an M.S.L.S. from the University of Tennessee at Knoxville and a B.A. in history from Michigan State University. He is the author of *IntroNet: A Beginner's Guide to Searching the Internet* (Neal-Schuman Publishers, 1999) and *Learning the Internet: A Workbook for Beginners* (Neal-Schuman Publishers, 1996). John can be reached via e-mail at *john. burke@uc.edu.*